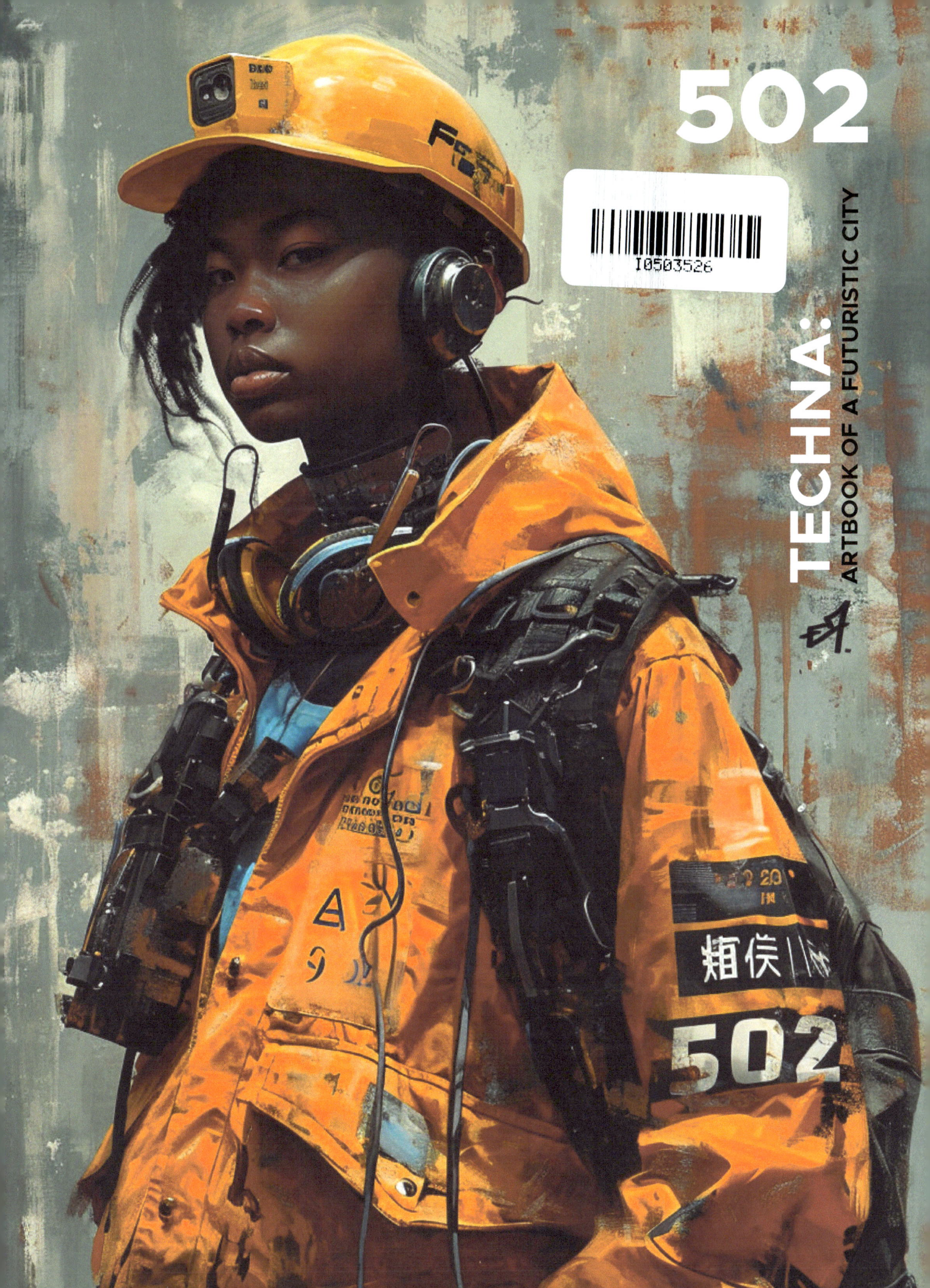

502

TECHNA:
ARTBOOK OF A FUTURISTIC CITY

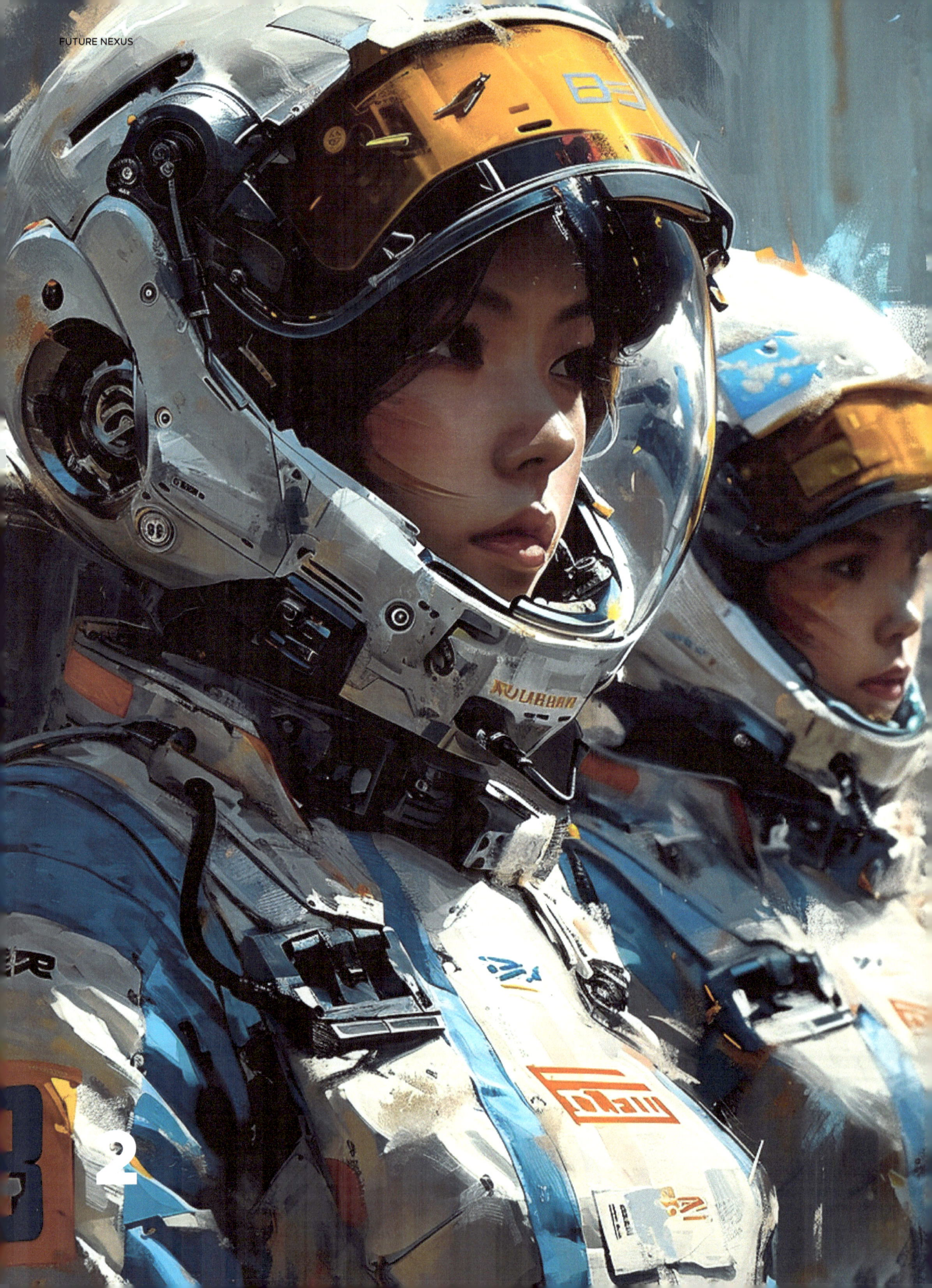

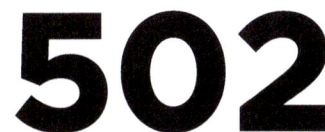

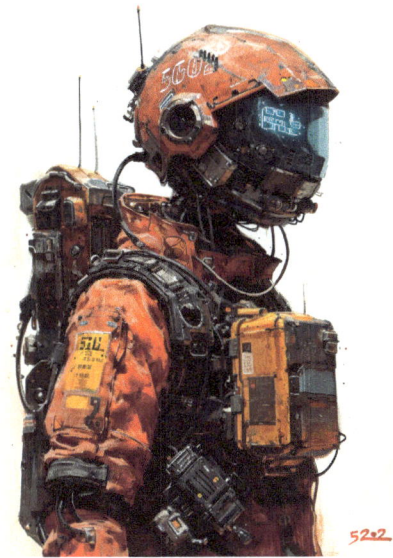

STORY

FUTURE NEXUS: THE CITY OF TECHNA

The city of Techna awakes to the hum of machinery and the buzz of workers preparing for another day. The colossal construction robots, known as Titan Units, are at the heart of the city's development. These AI-enhanced machines, with their insect-inspired heads and heavy-duty frames, are indispensable in building and maintaining the towering structures that define Techna's skyline. Today, Unit 5002 is tasked with reinforcing the foundation of a new skyscraper, its operators coordinating every movement with precision and expertise.

Amid the mechanical giants, the human workers of Techna play a crucial role. Among them is Hana, a skilled technician and operator. With her advanced suit equipped with AR displays and communication devices, Hana oversees the programming and repair of the Titan Units. Her dedication and skill are evident in the seamless operation of the machinery around her. Today, Hana is troubleshooting a minor glitch in Unit 502, ensuring it remains operational throughout the day's demanding tasks.

The Heavylift units, like the Titan Unit 502, are designed for the most challenging tasks. These behemoths can lift and transport materials that would be impossible for human workers alone. In the heart of Techna's industrial district, these machines are the backbone of the city's rapid expansion. Workers like Hana coordinate the efforts, ensuring that every piece of material is placed with pinpoint accuracy. Today's task involves relocating a massive steel beam, a job that requires both human ingenuity and robotic strength.

Even in a city as advanced as Techna, the human element remains essential. Breaks are a necessary respite for the workers who operate and maintain the city's technological marvels. As Hana takes a moment to rest, she reflects on the progress made and the challenges ahead. The camaraderie among the workers is palpable, each one understanding the importance of their role in building the future.

The Overseers are the project managers and coordinators of Techna's construction efforts. Equipped with the latest in wearable technology, they ensure that every project runs smoothly and on schedule. Today, the Over-

3

seers are inspecting the progress on a new transportation hub, a critical addition to the city's infrastructure. Their advanced suits allow them to access real-time data and communicate with both human workers and AI systems, ensuring seamless integration of efforts.

Beyond construction, Techna is also a hub for innovation in transportation. The city hosts an annual race that showcases the latest in vehicular technology. The racing teams are comprised of engineers, designers, and drivers who push the limits of speed and performance. Today, the Nexus Racing Team is preparing for a test run, their state-of-the-art vehicle embodying the cutting-edge advancements of the era. The team's collaborative efforts and technological prowess make them a formidable competitor in the race to come.

The streets of Techna are a testament to the city's harmonious blend of technology and humanity. The Titan Units walk among the citizens, their presence a reminder of the city's relentless drive towards progress. The bright blue sky overhead contrasts with the bustling activity below, creating a scene of dynamic energy and vibrant life. As Hana and her team navigate the streets, they prepare for another day of groundbreaking work, ready to face whatever challenges lie ahead.

The Pioneers of Techna are the innovators and visionaries who drive the city's progress. Their latest project involves developing a new type of transportation vehicle, one that promises to revolutionize urban mobility. As Hana and her team unveil the prototype, the excitement is palpable. The crowd gathers to witness the future in action, a testament to Techna's spirit of innovation and its commitment to creating a better tomorrow.

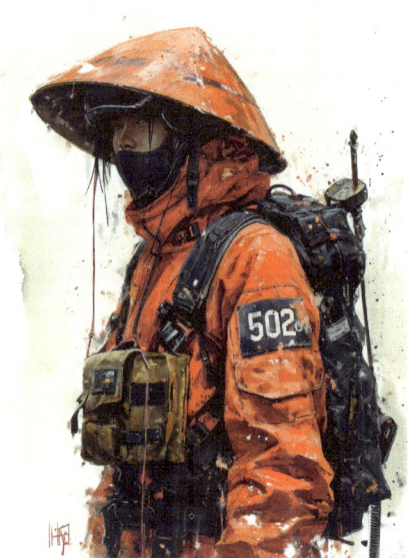
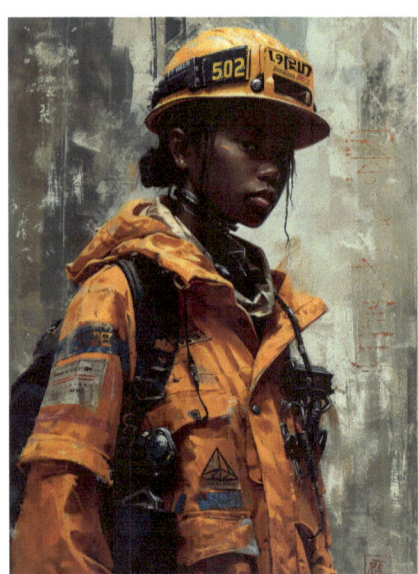

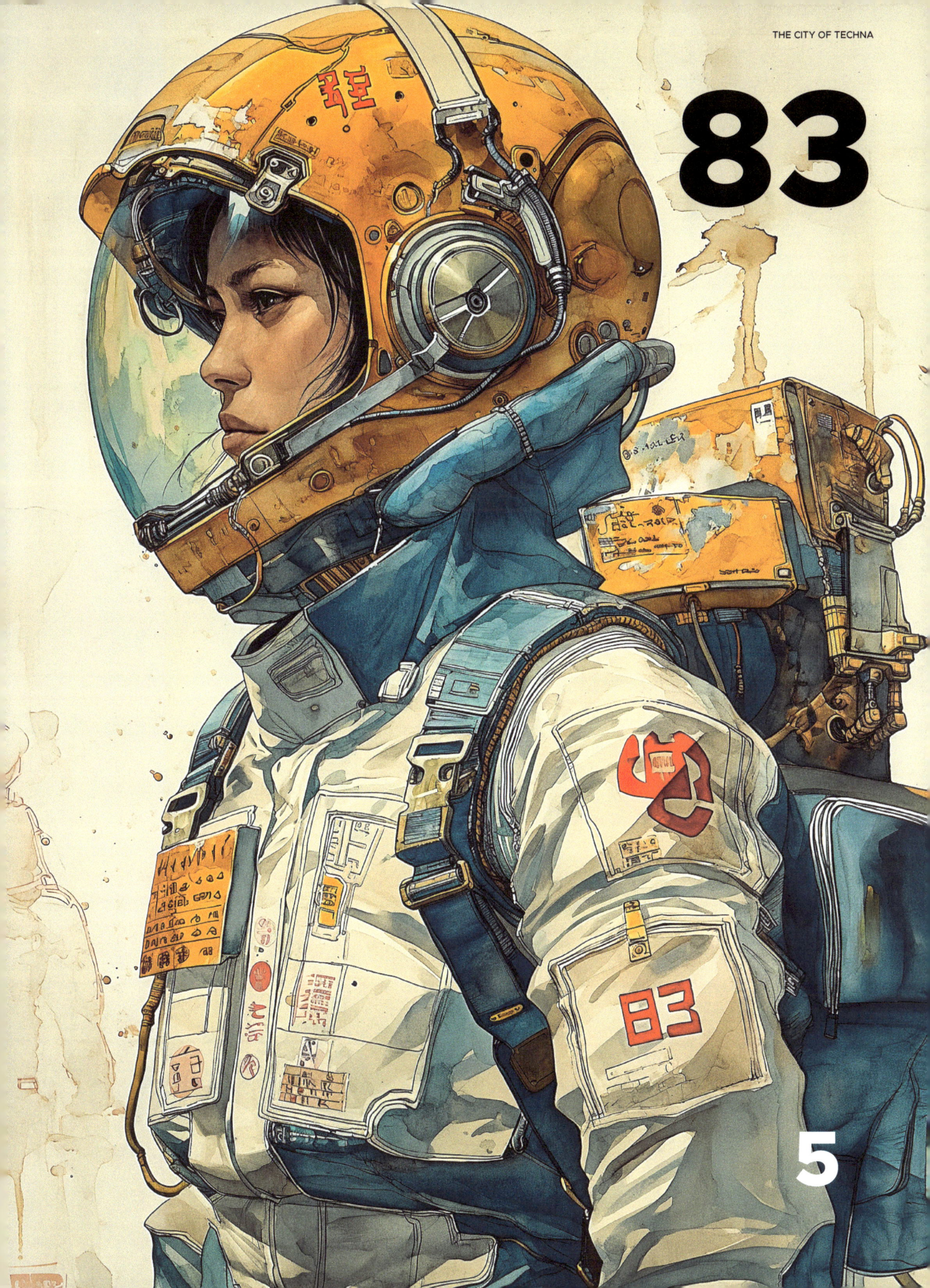

83

83

5

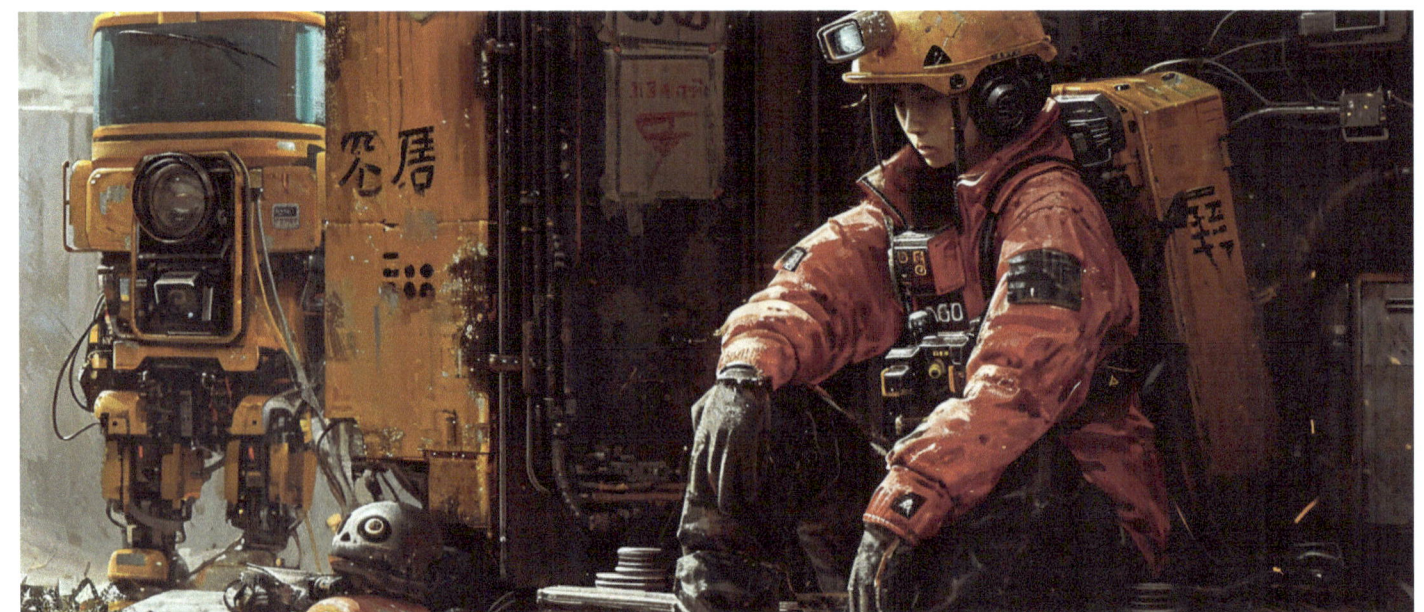

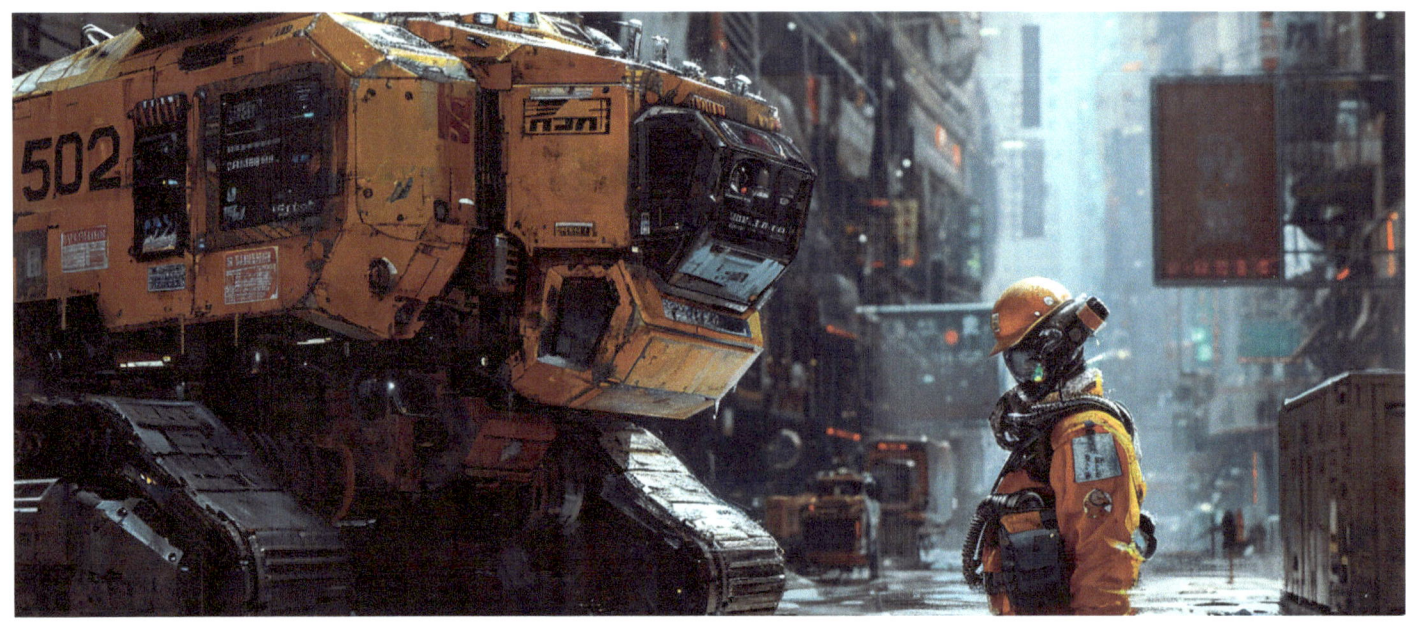

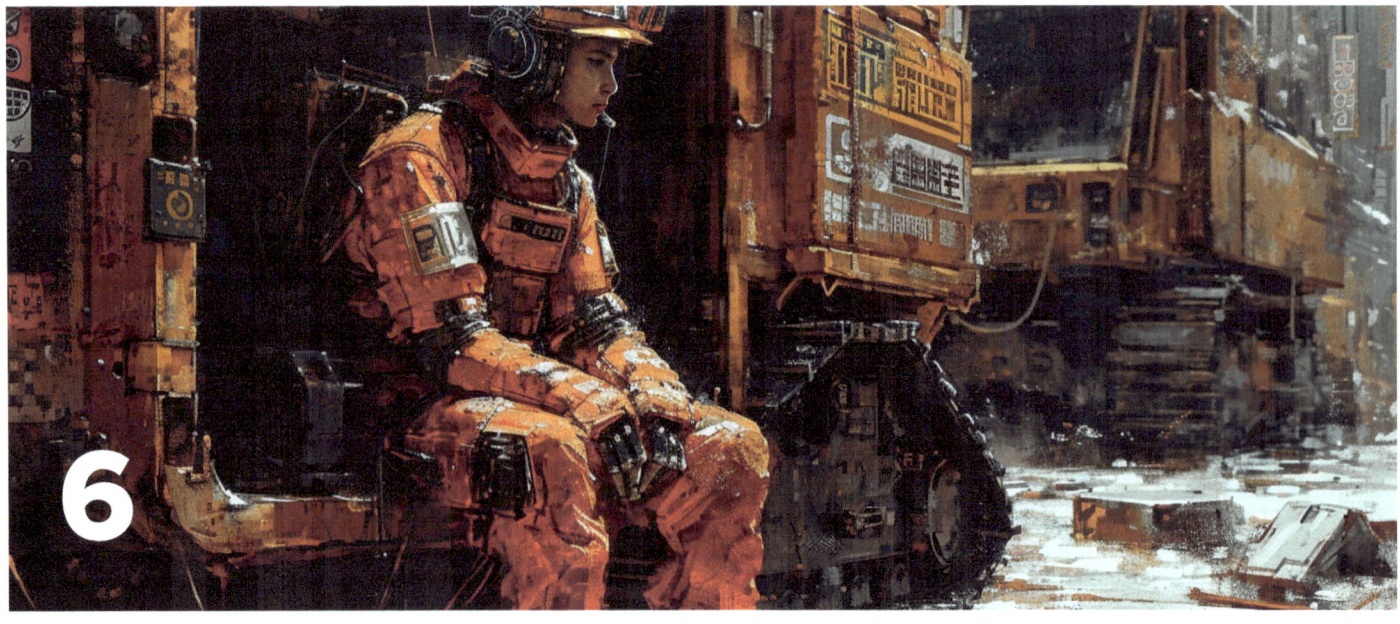

6

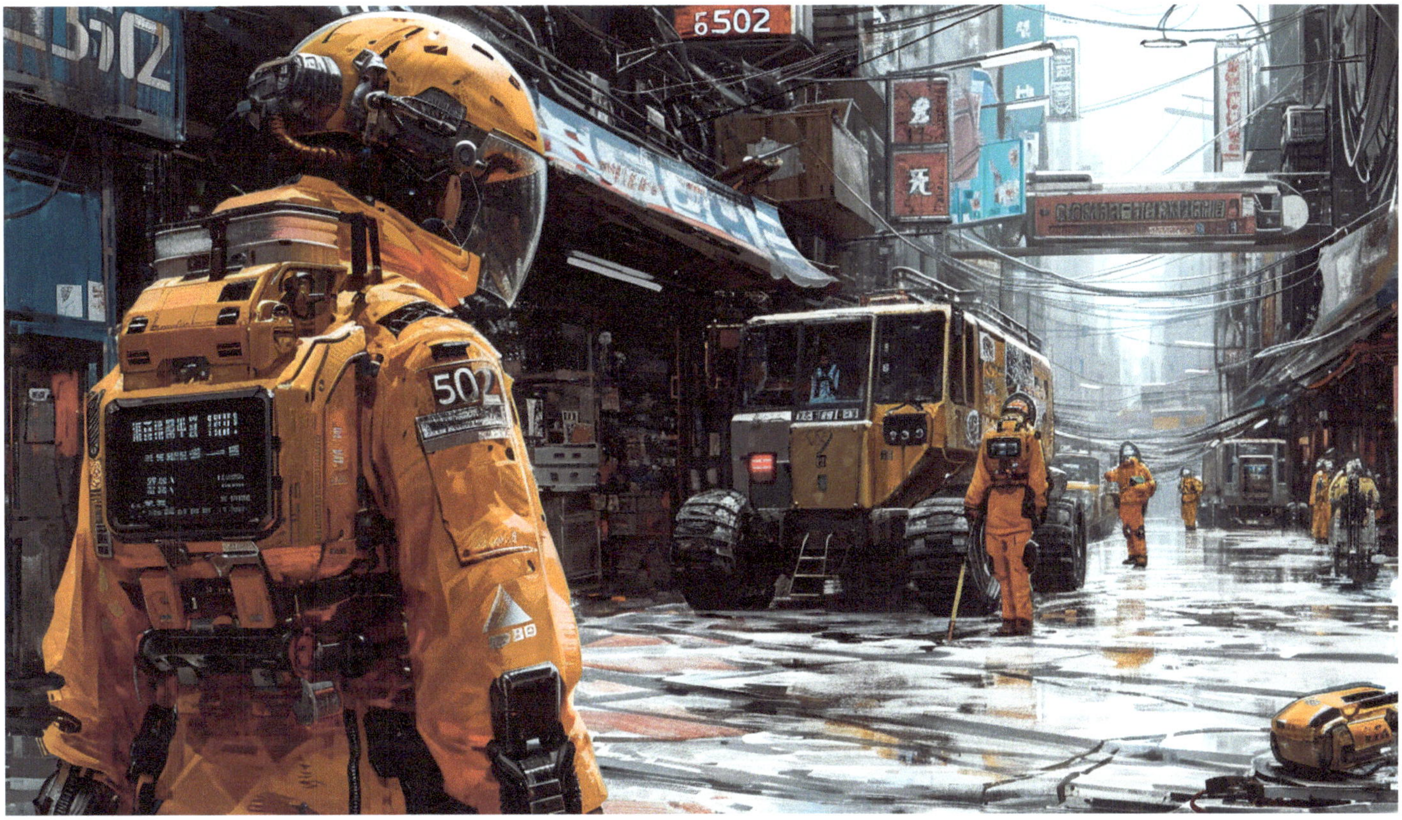

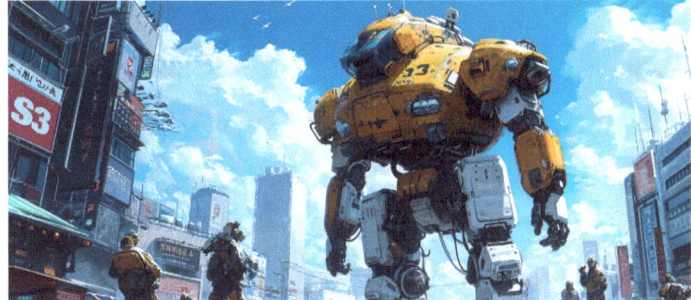

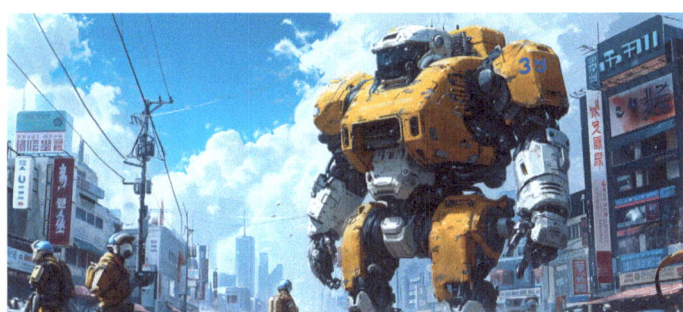

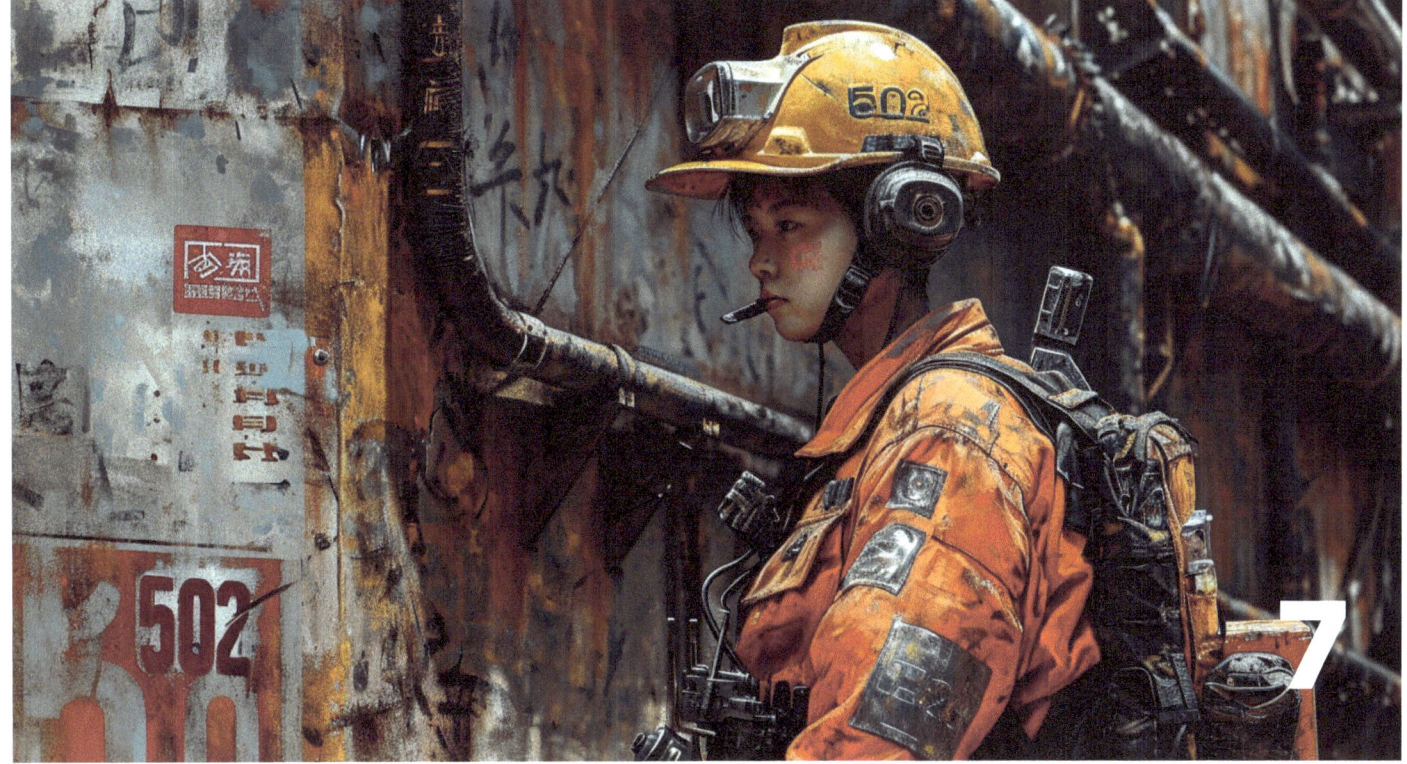

7

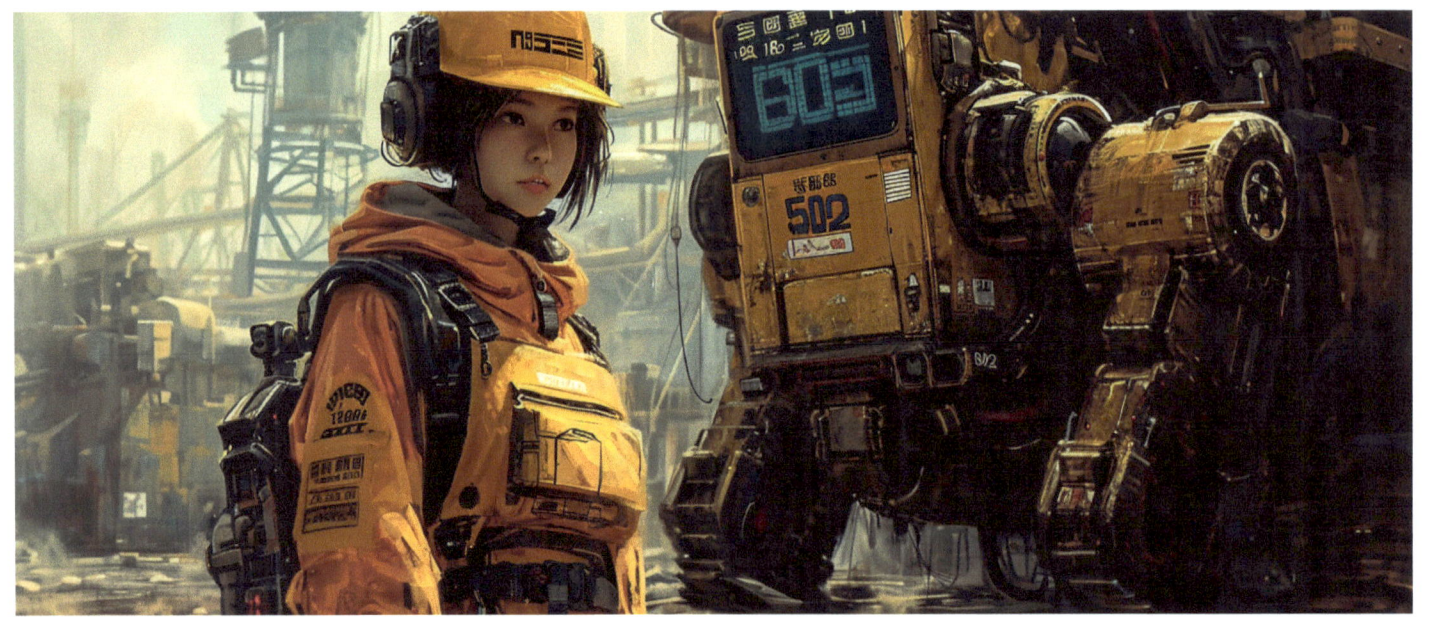

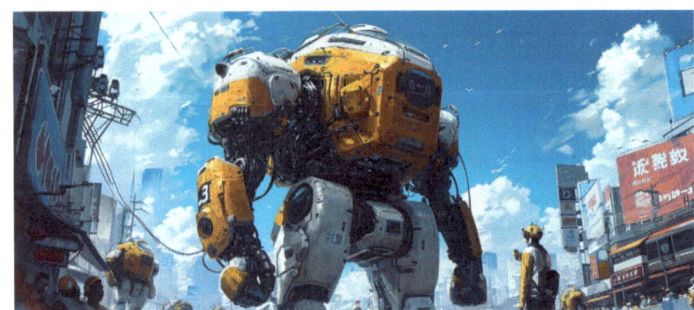

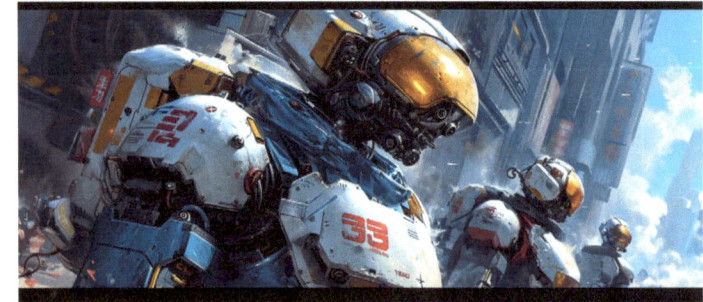

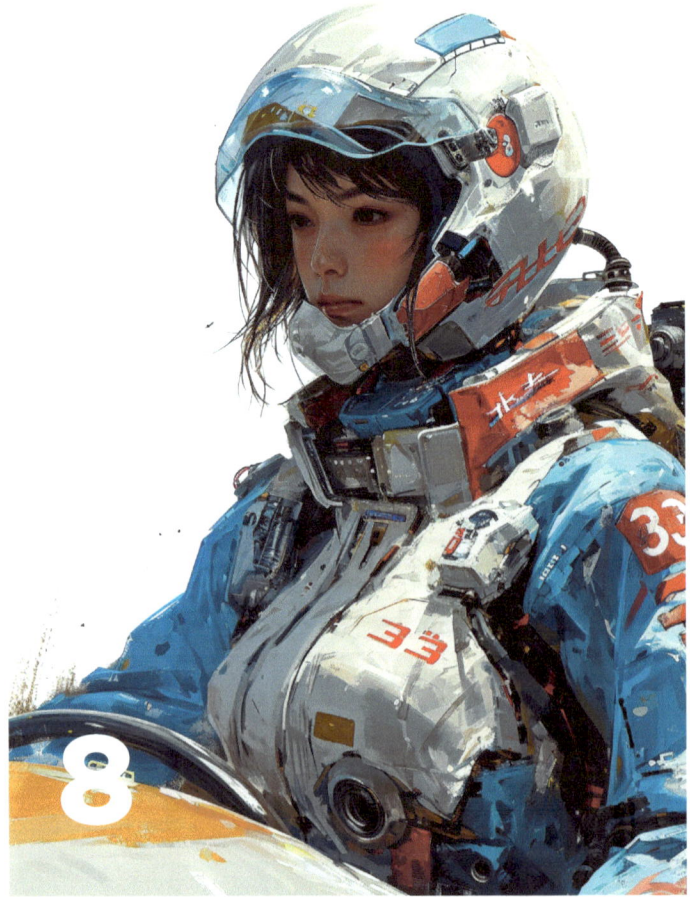

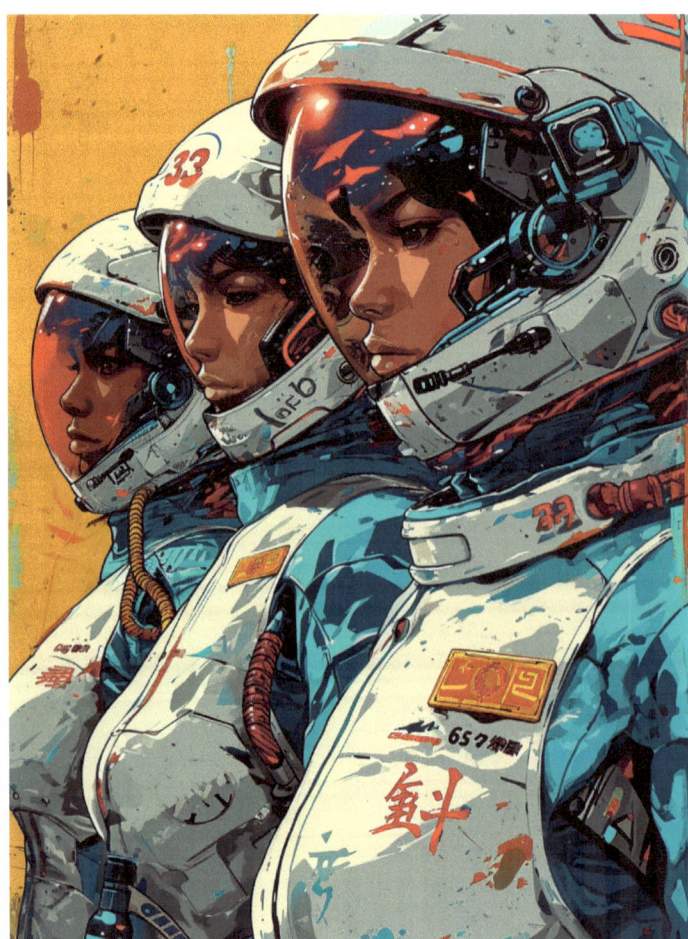

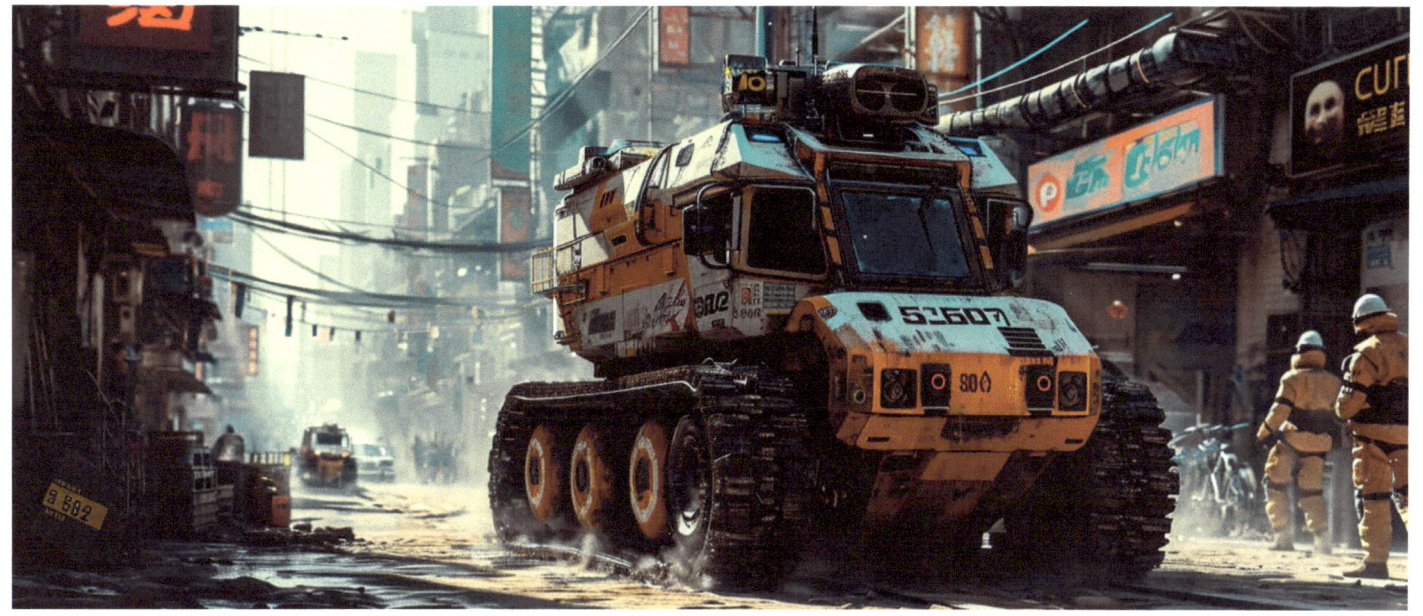

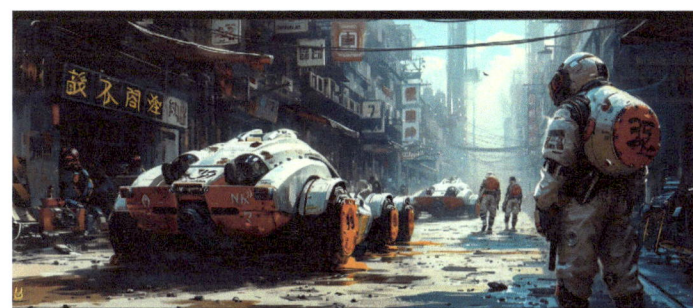

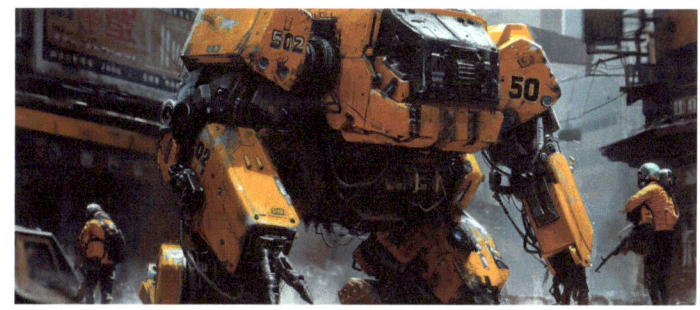

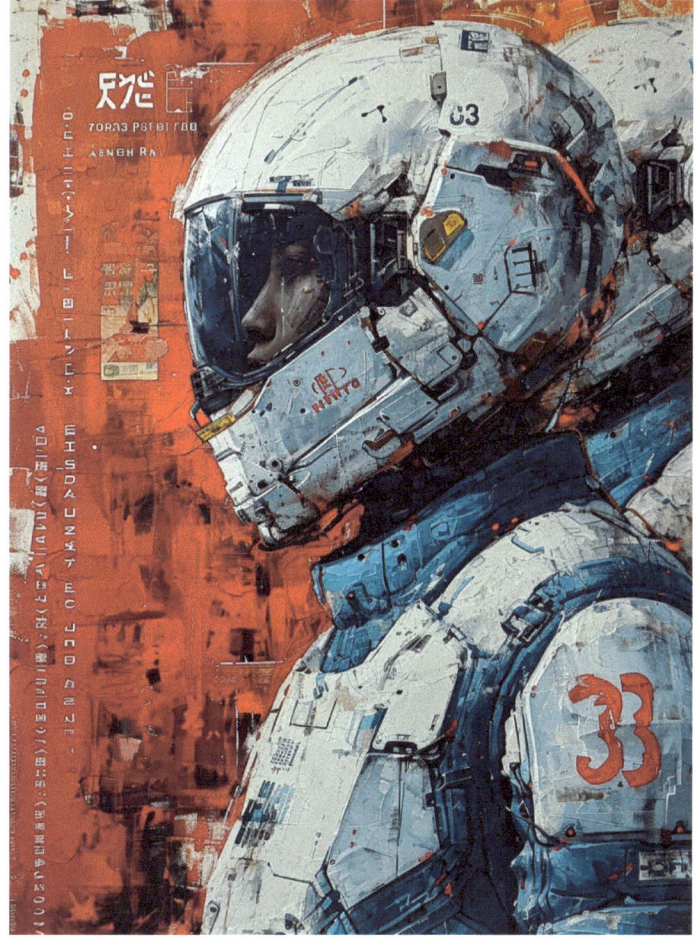

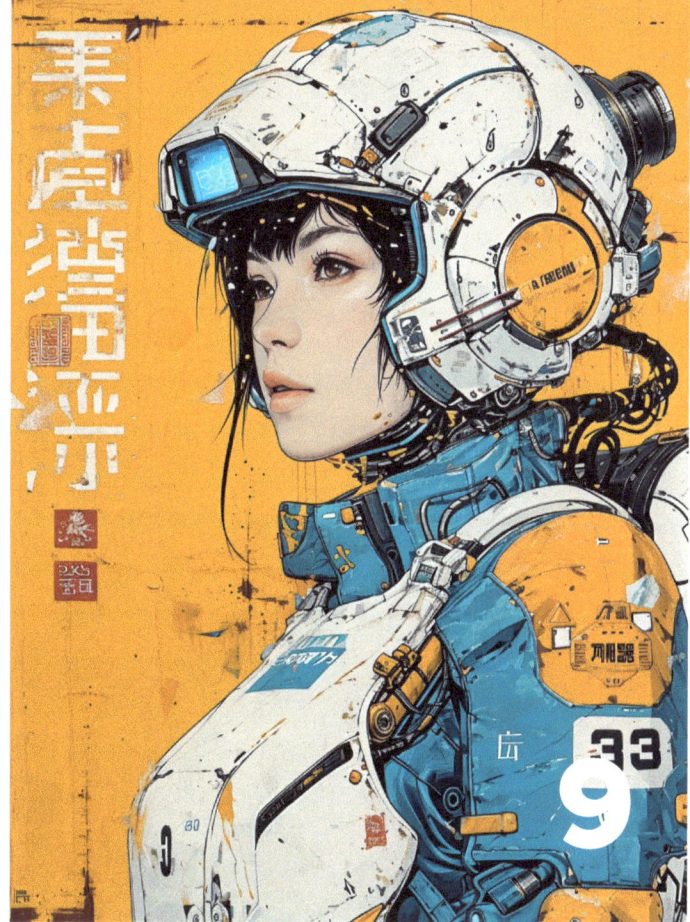

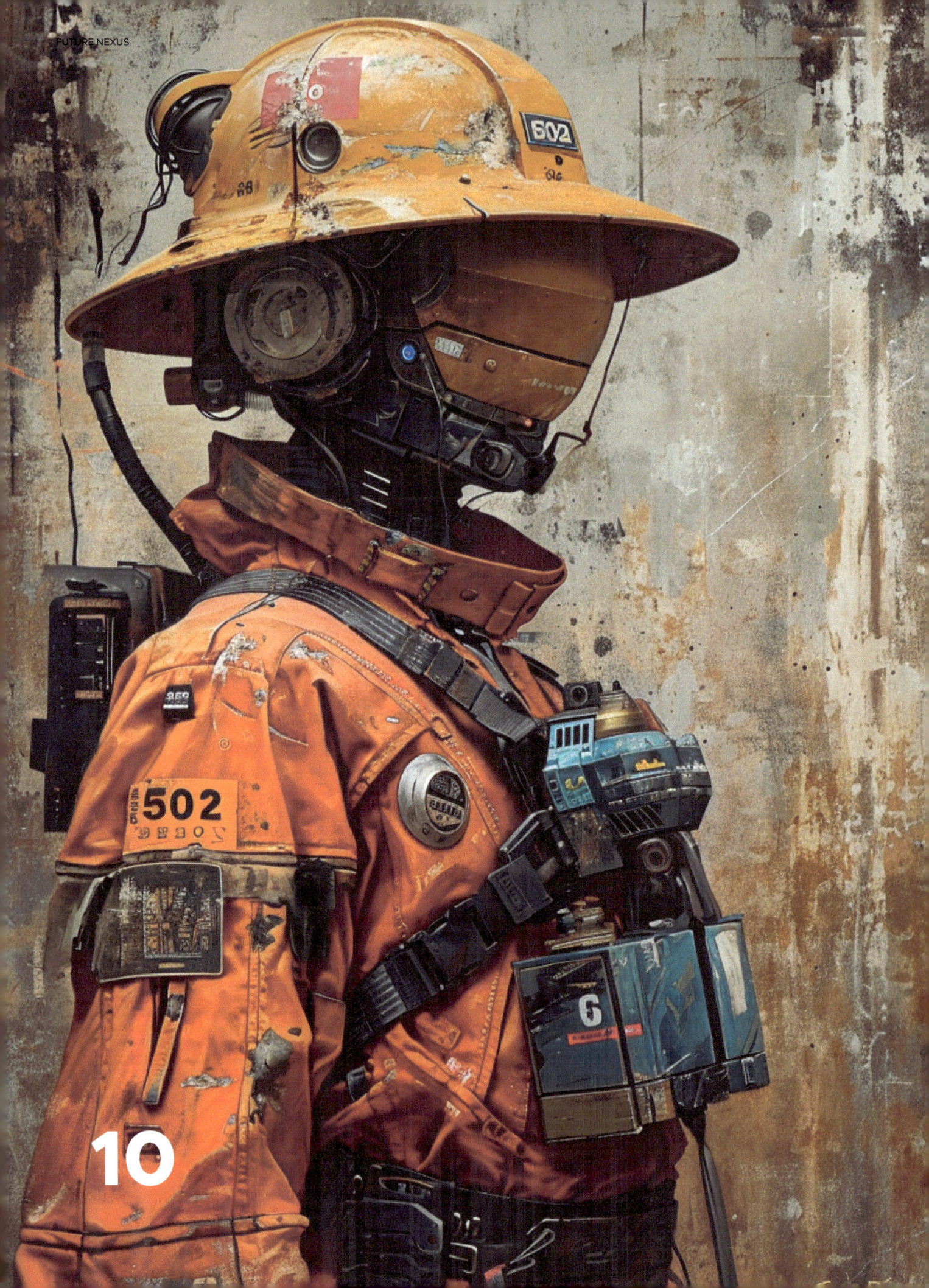

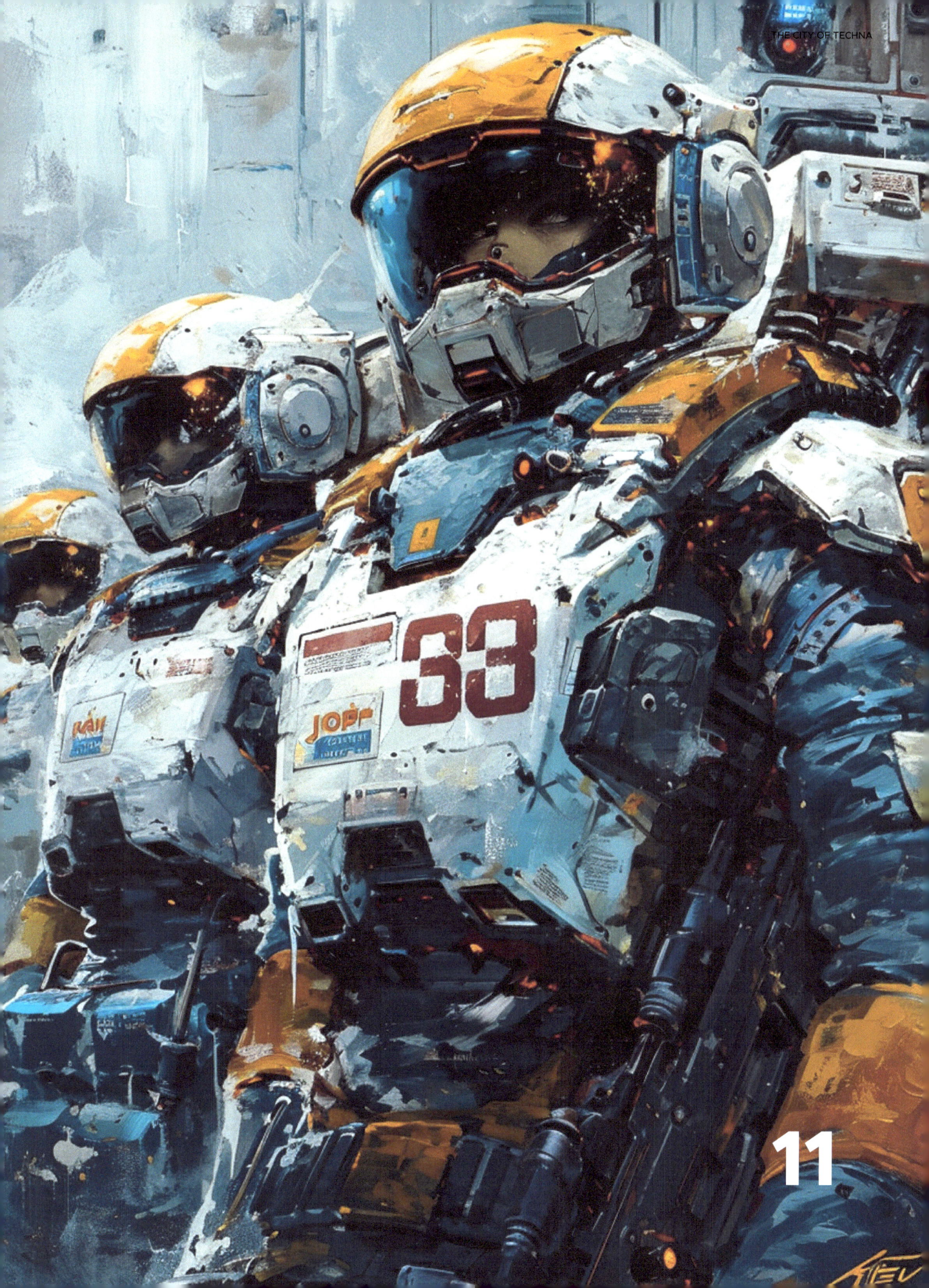

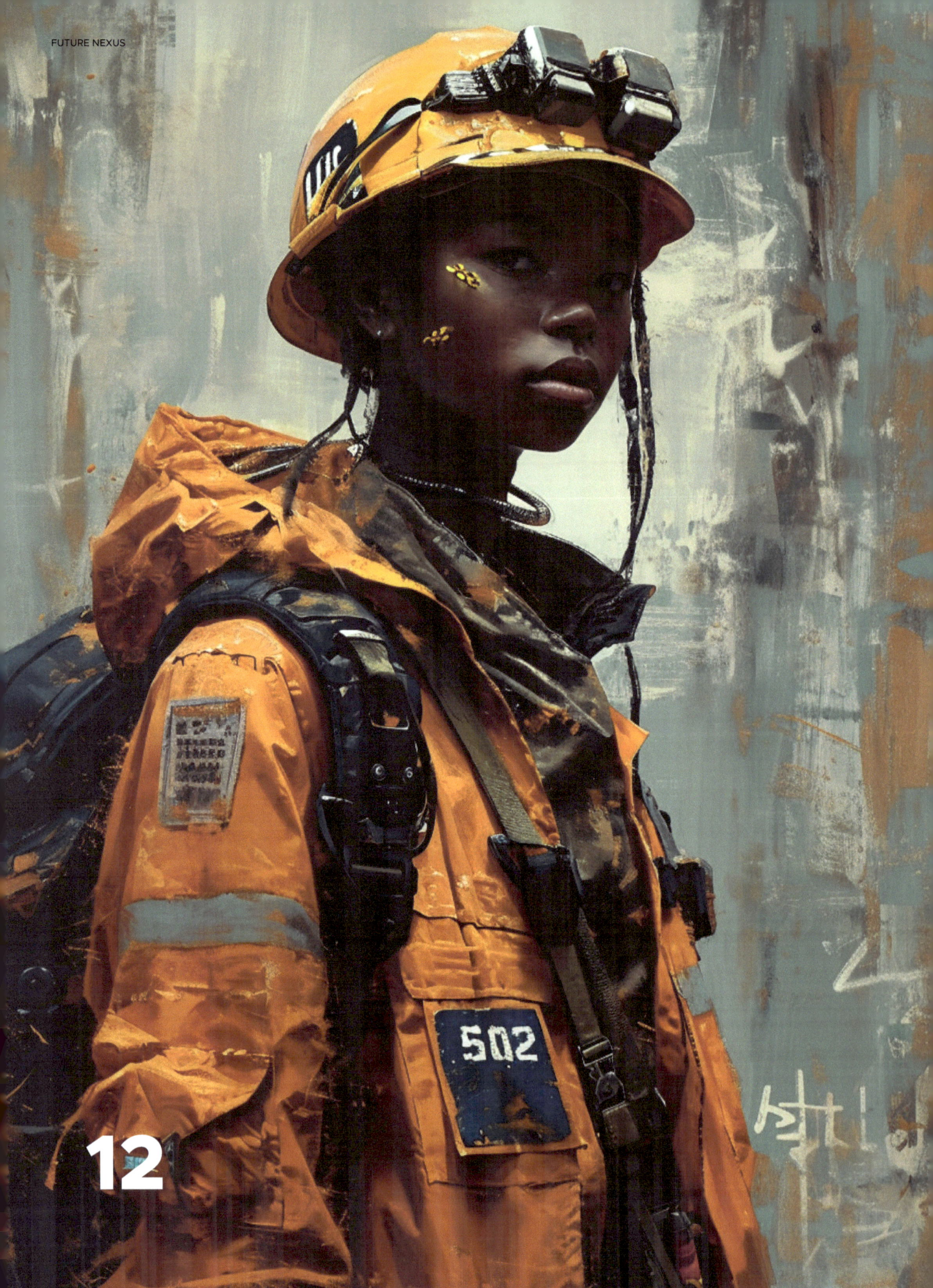

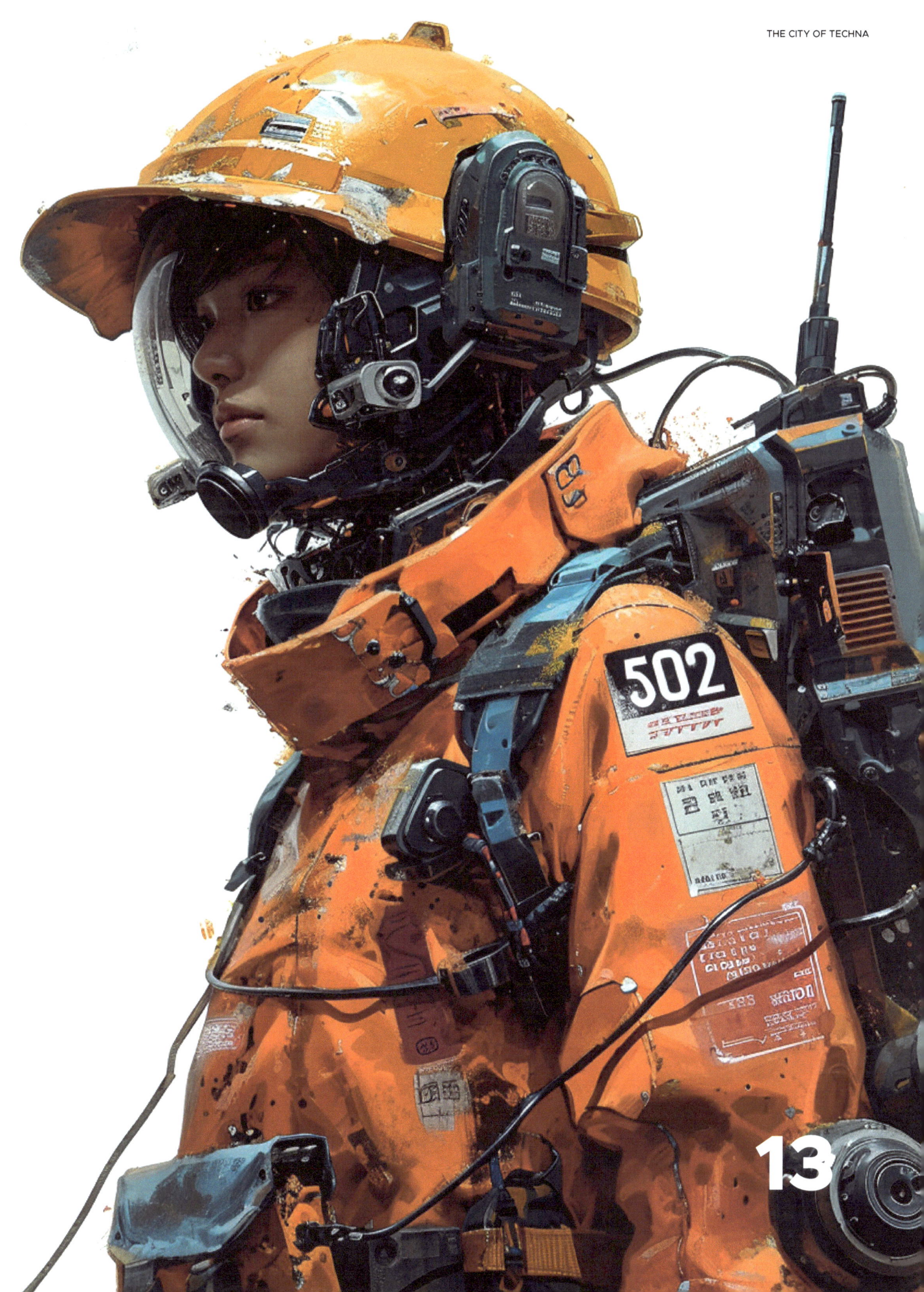

13

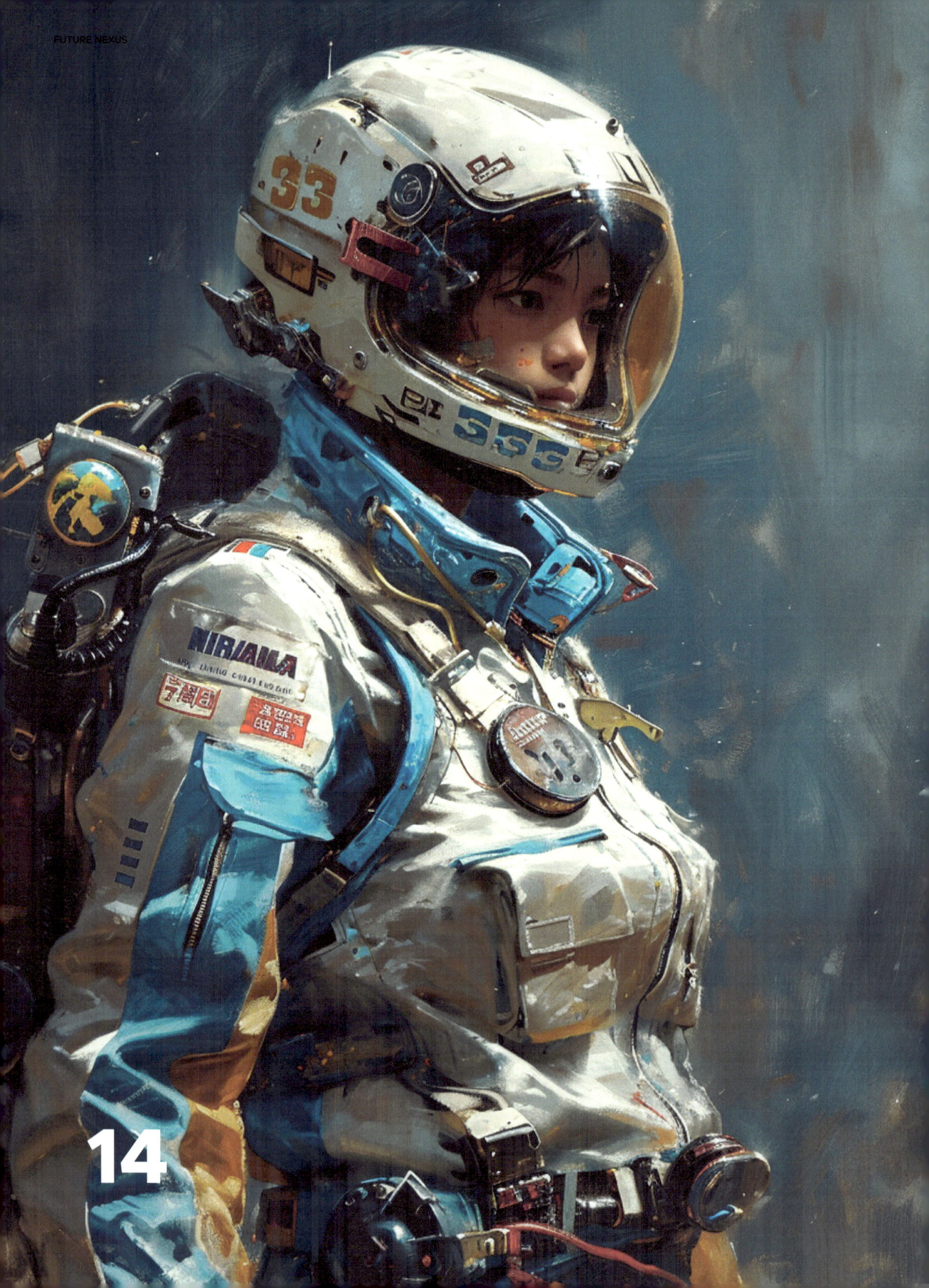

14

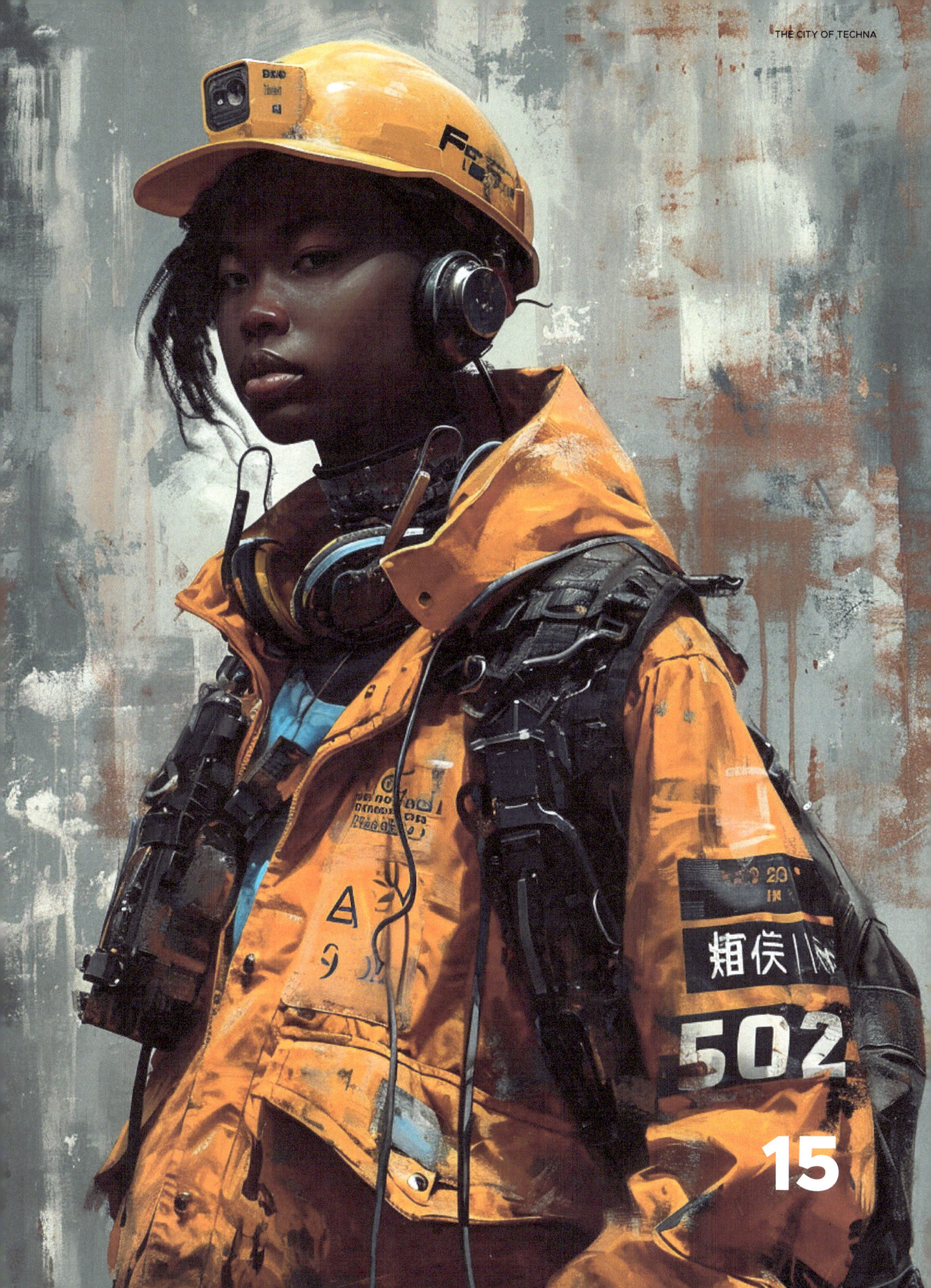

15

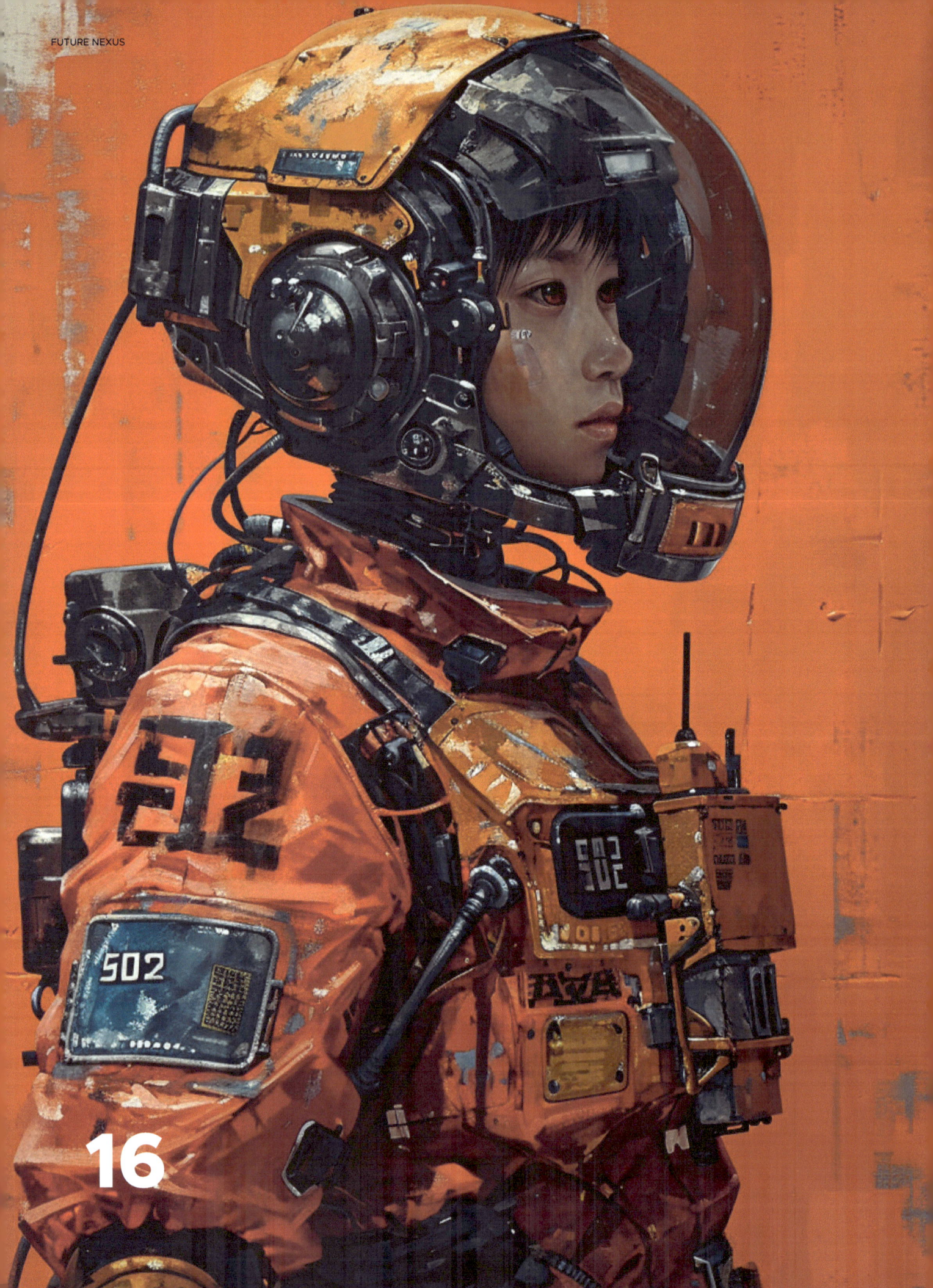

16

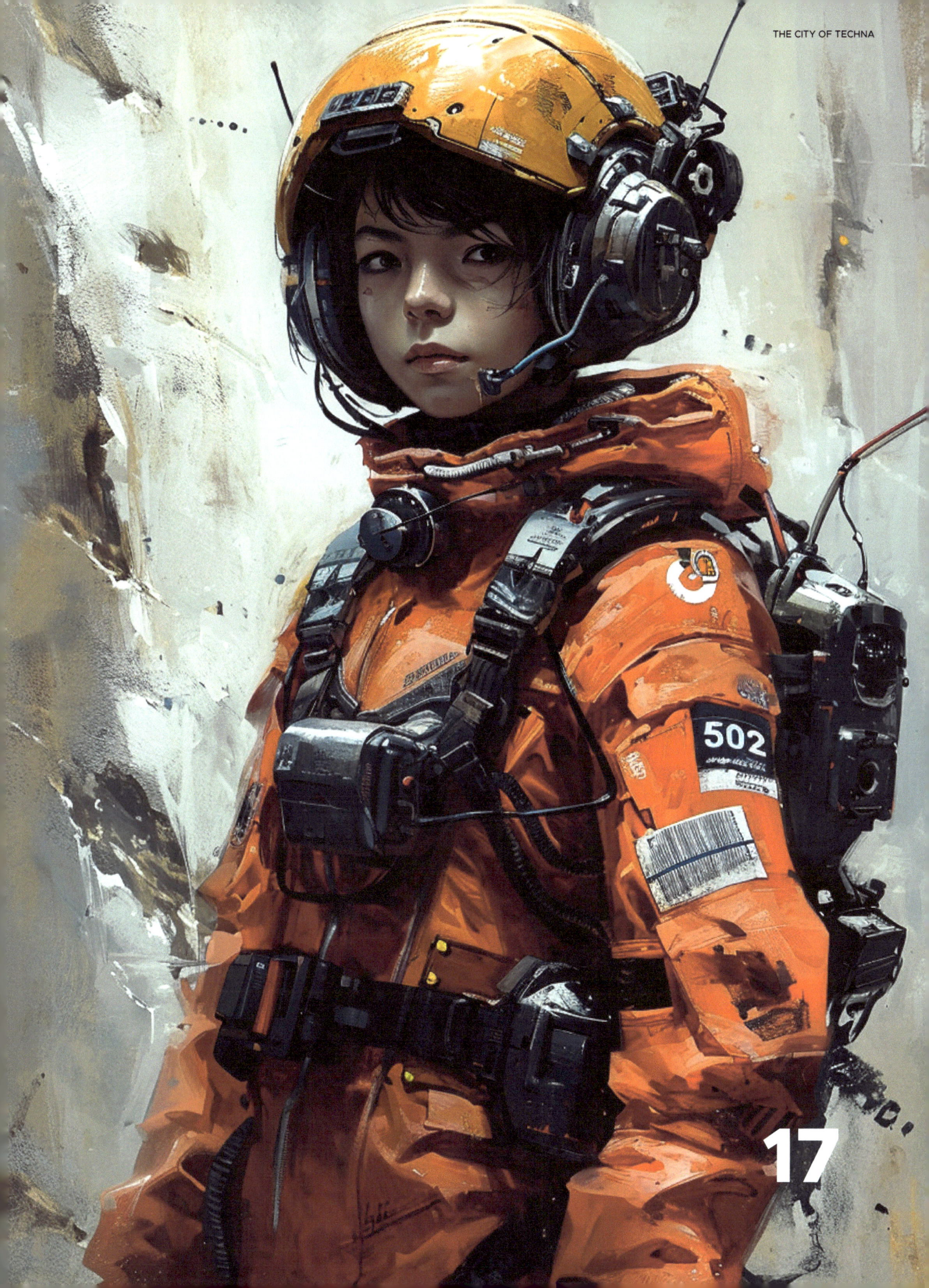

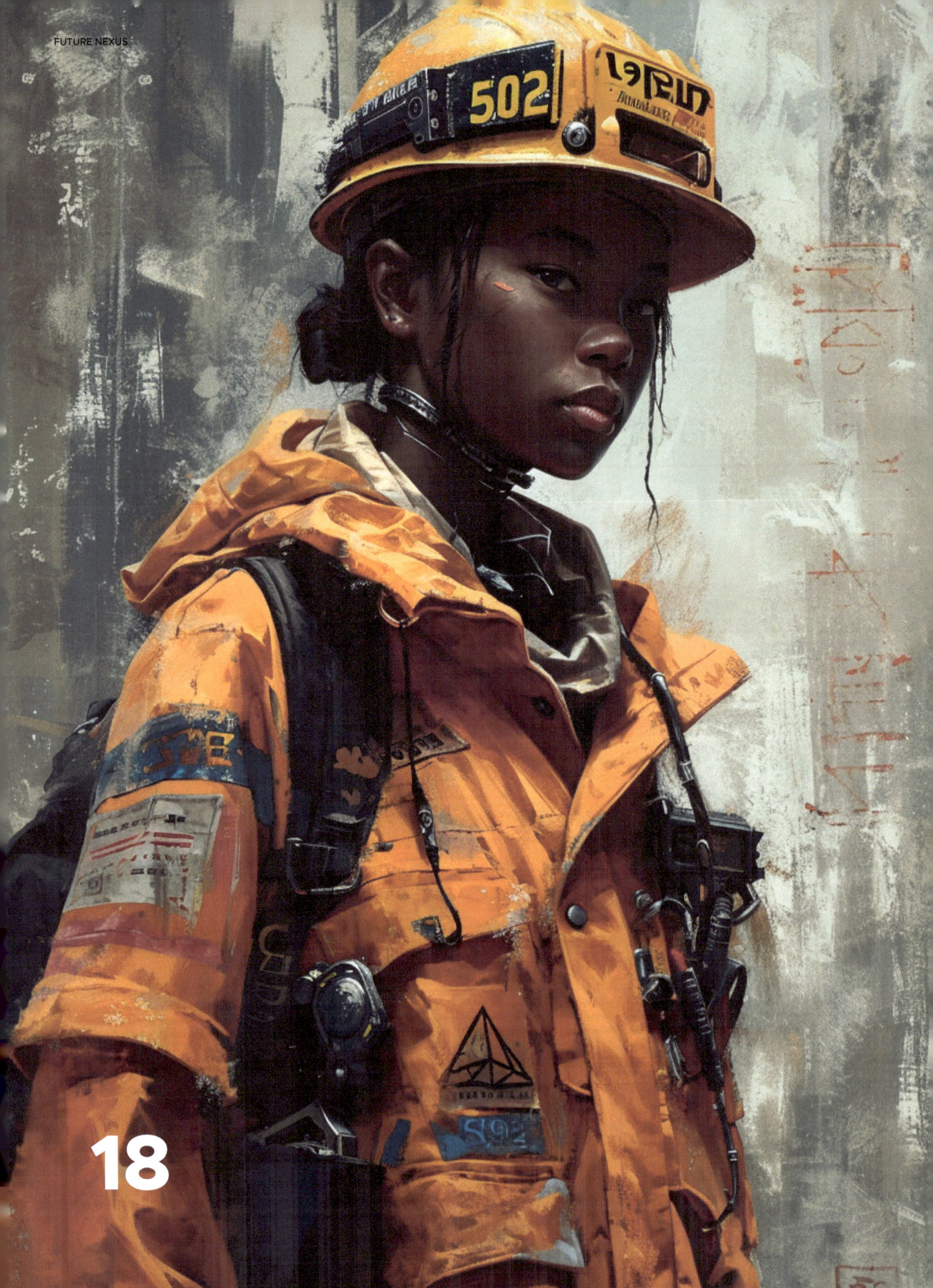

18

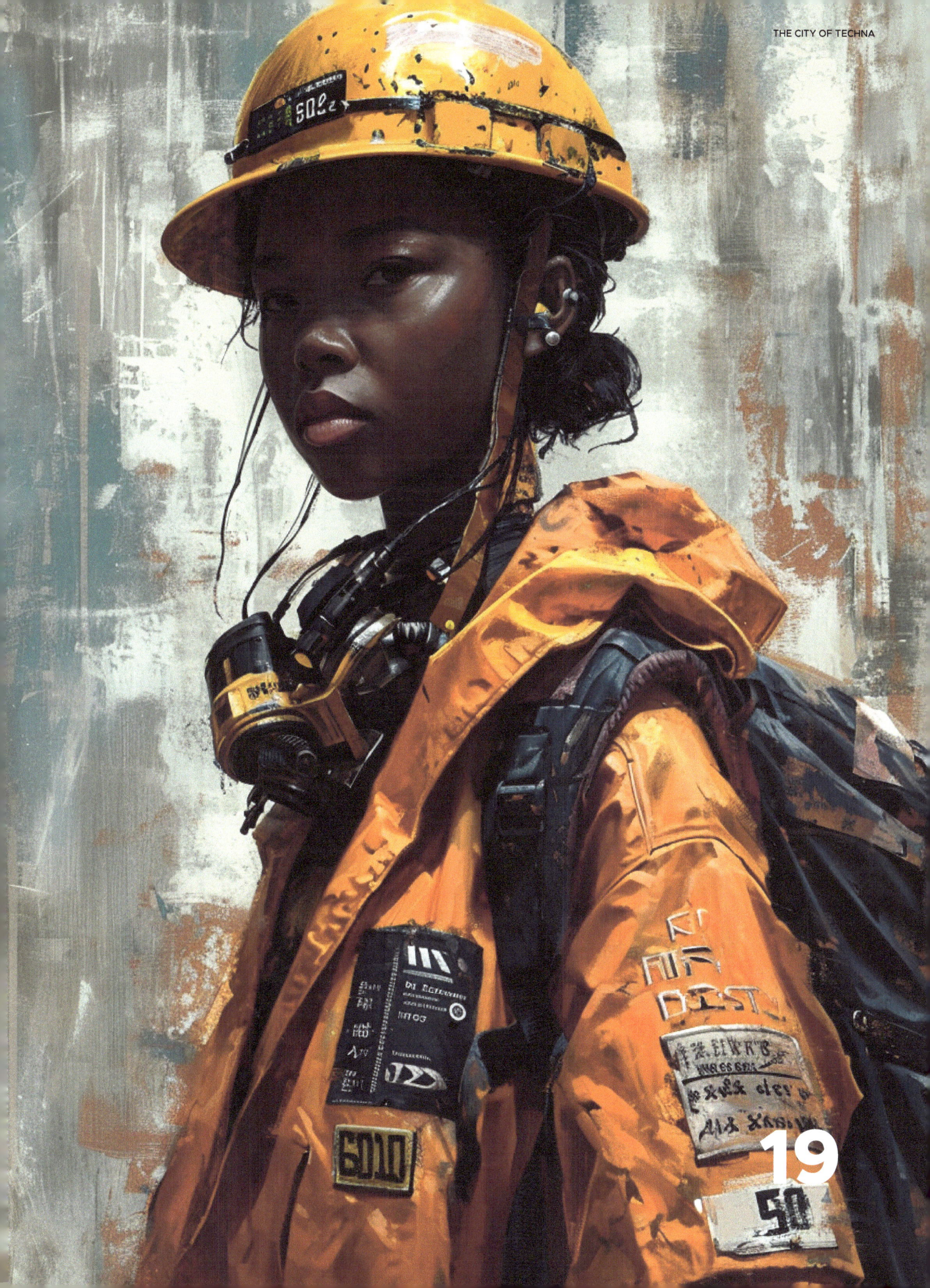

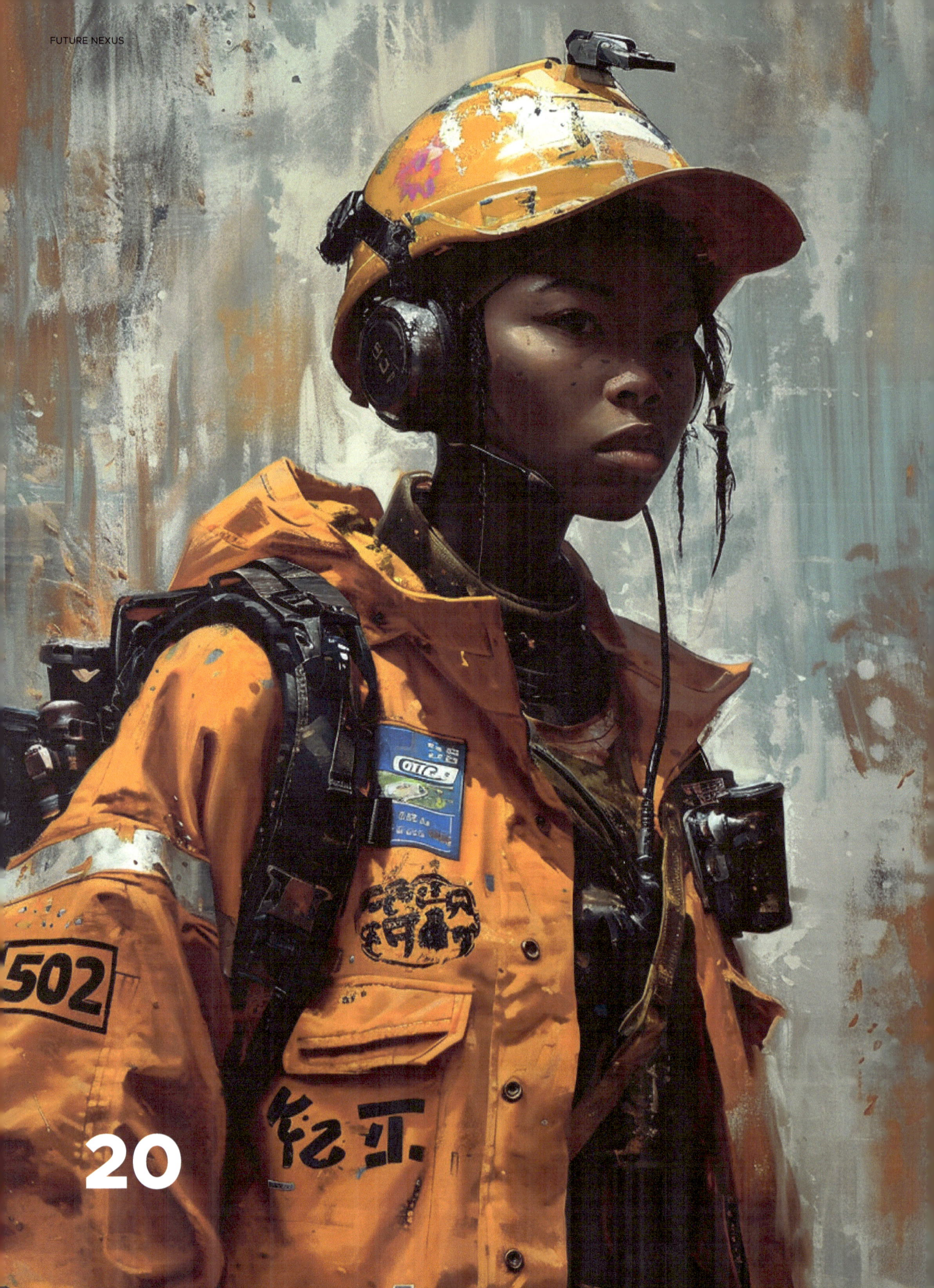

20

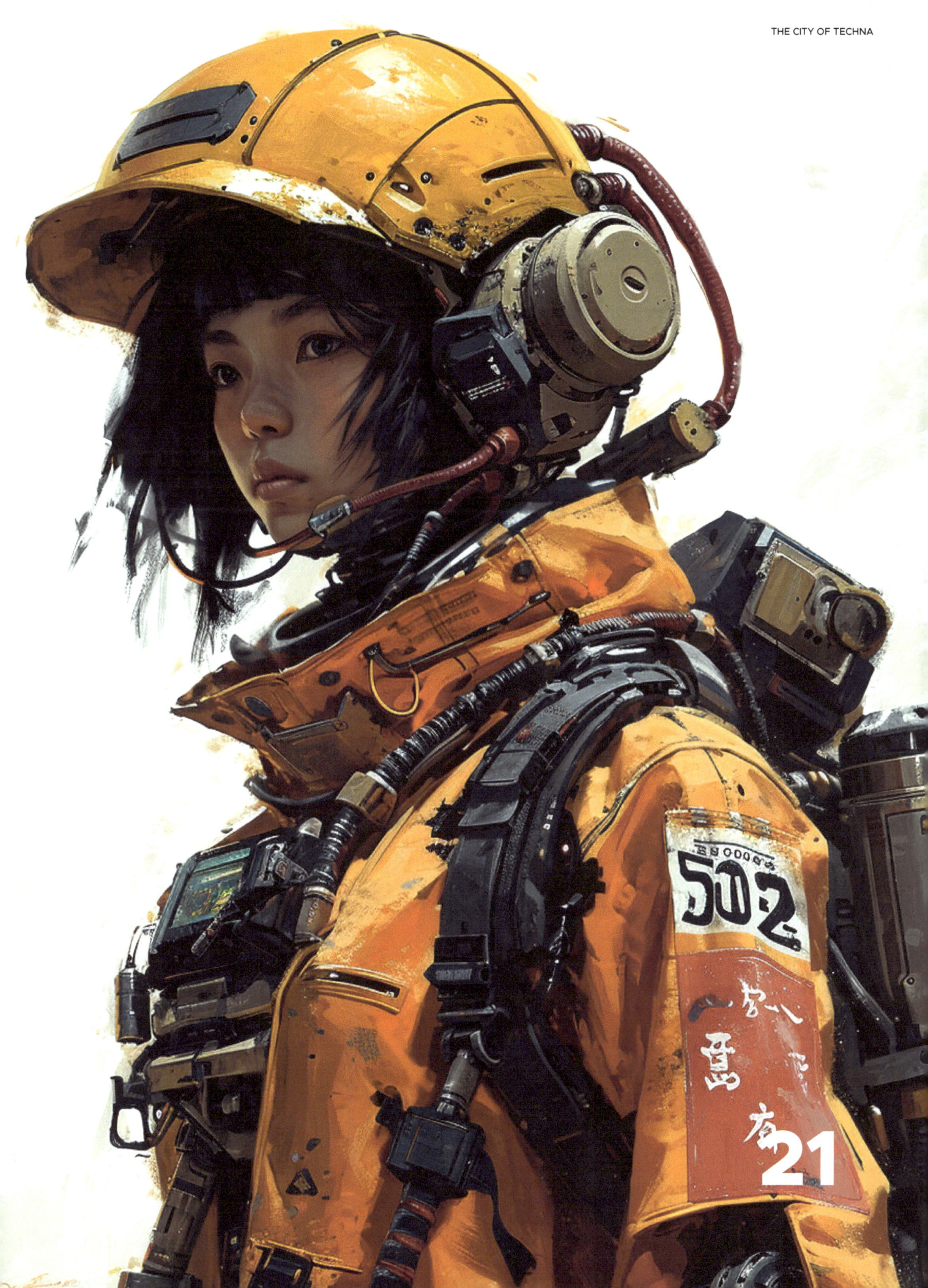

21

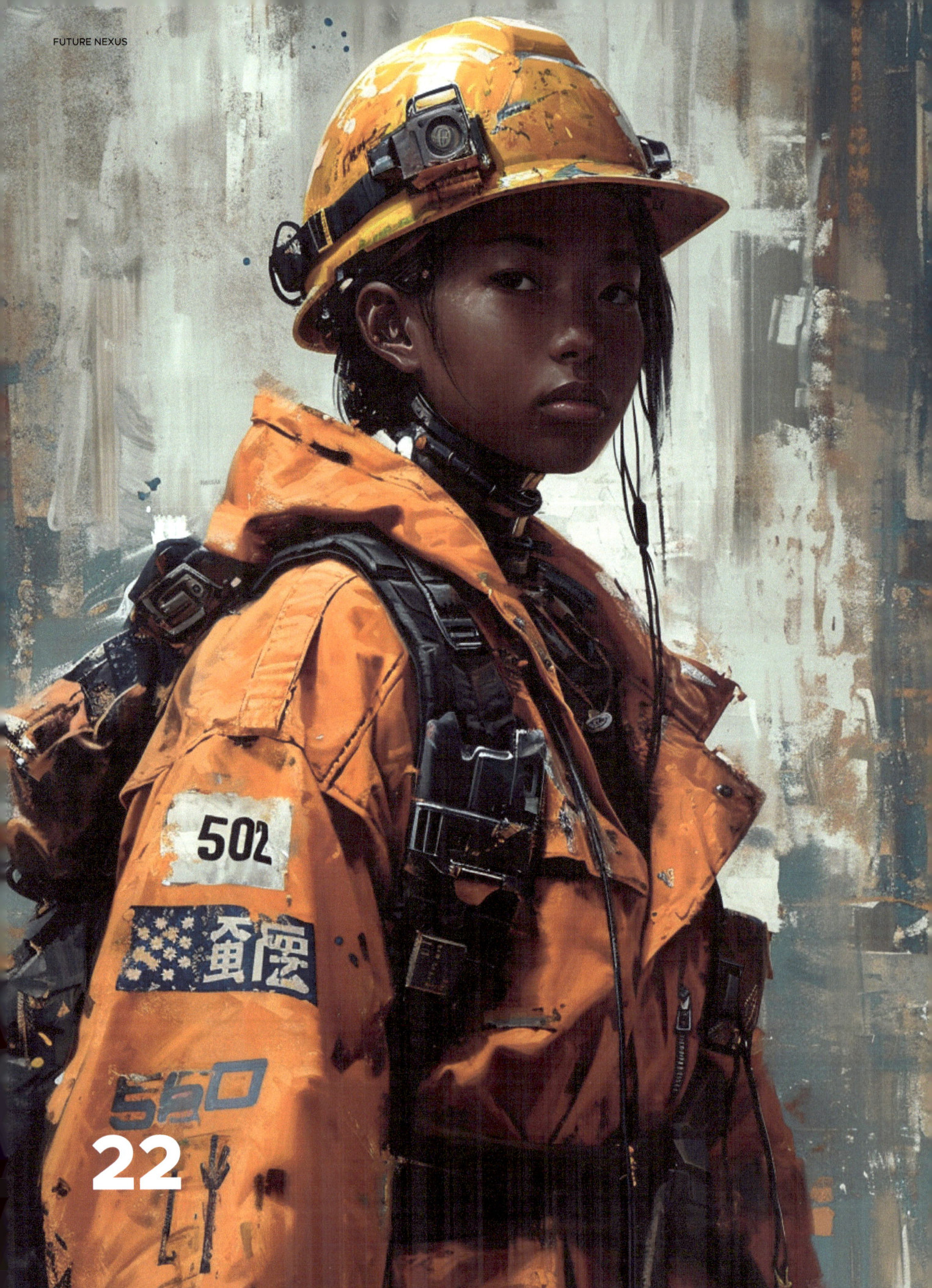

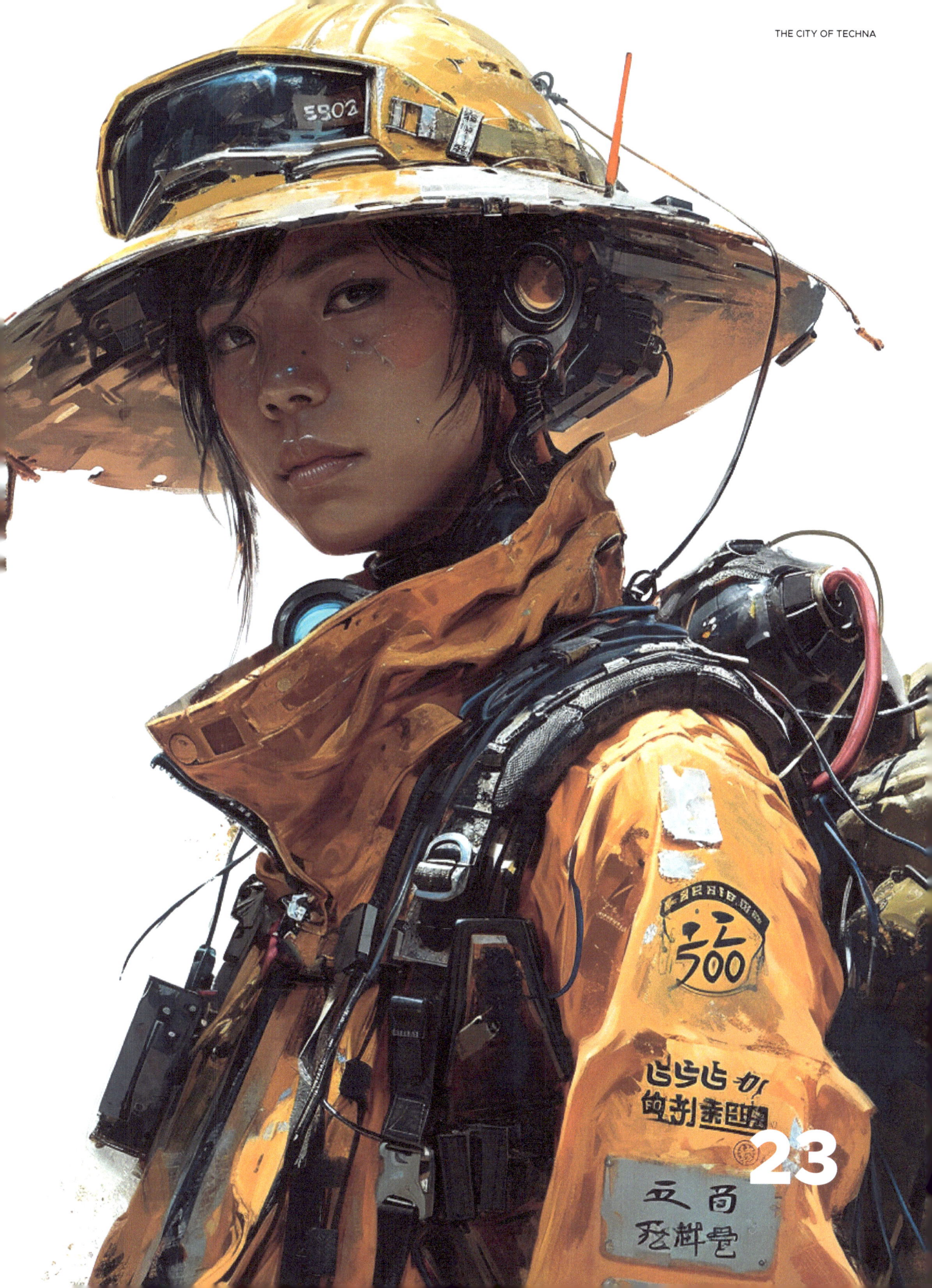

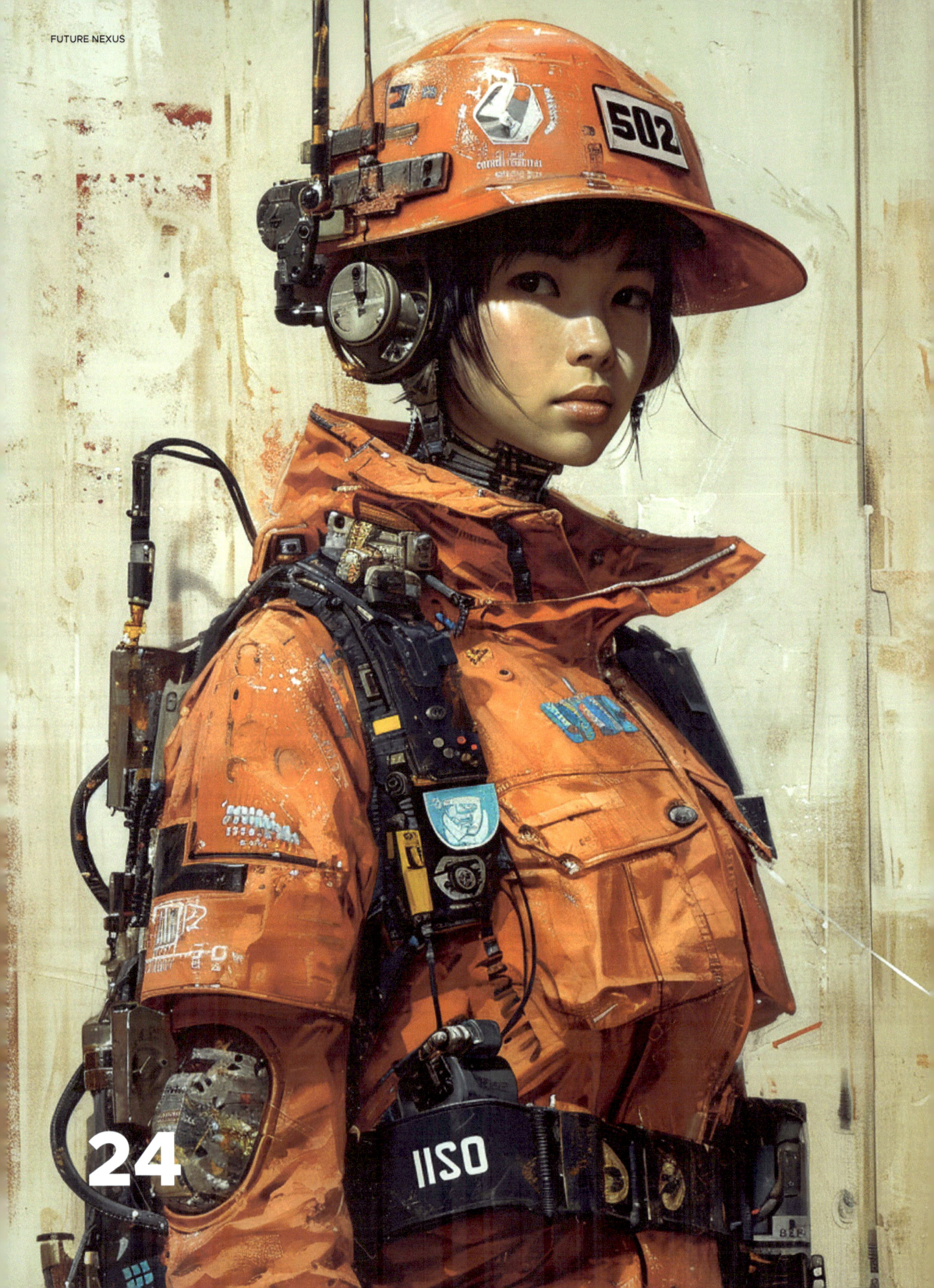

24

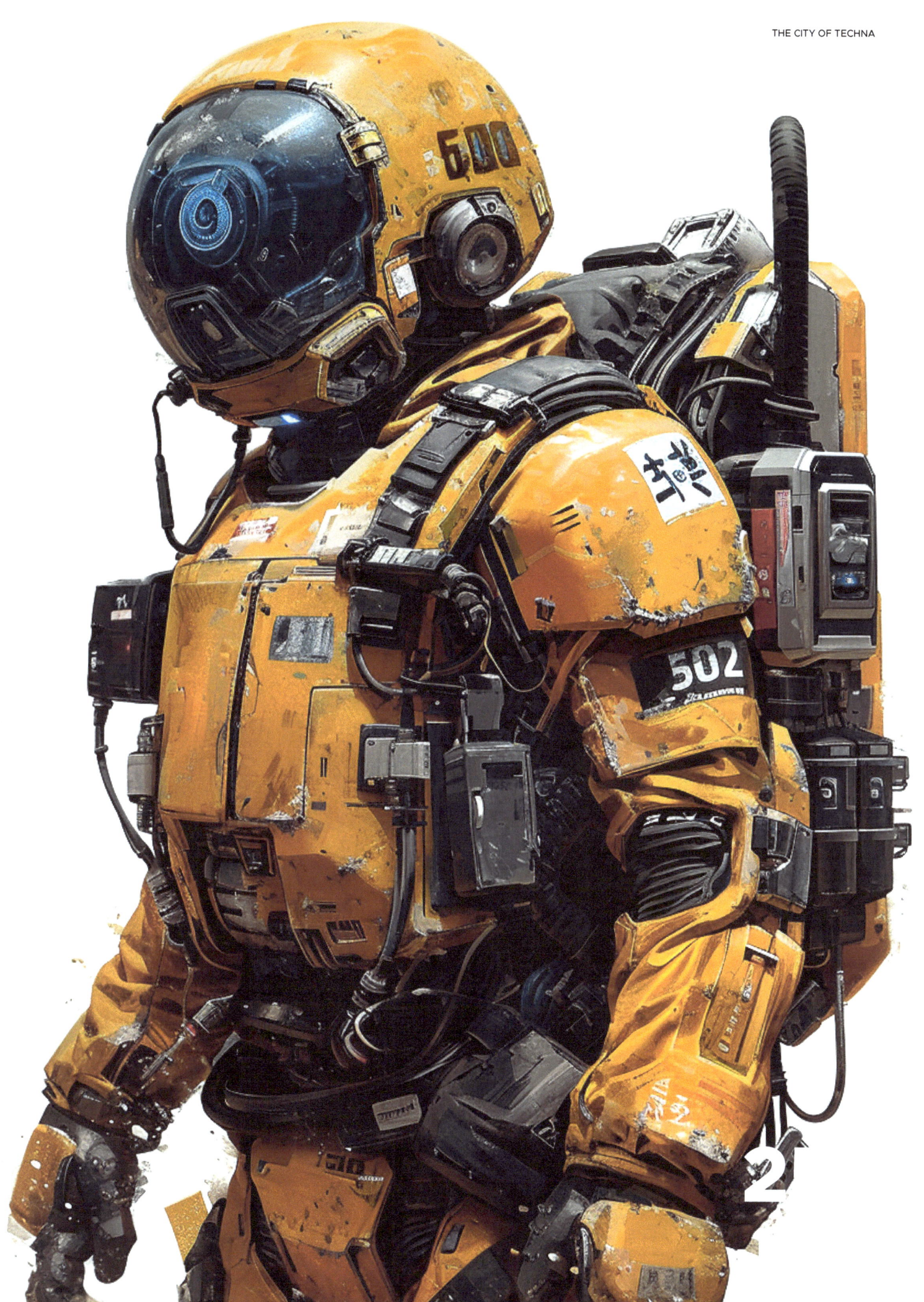

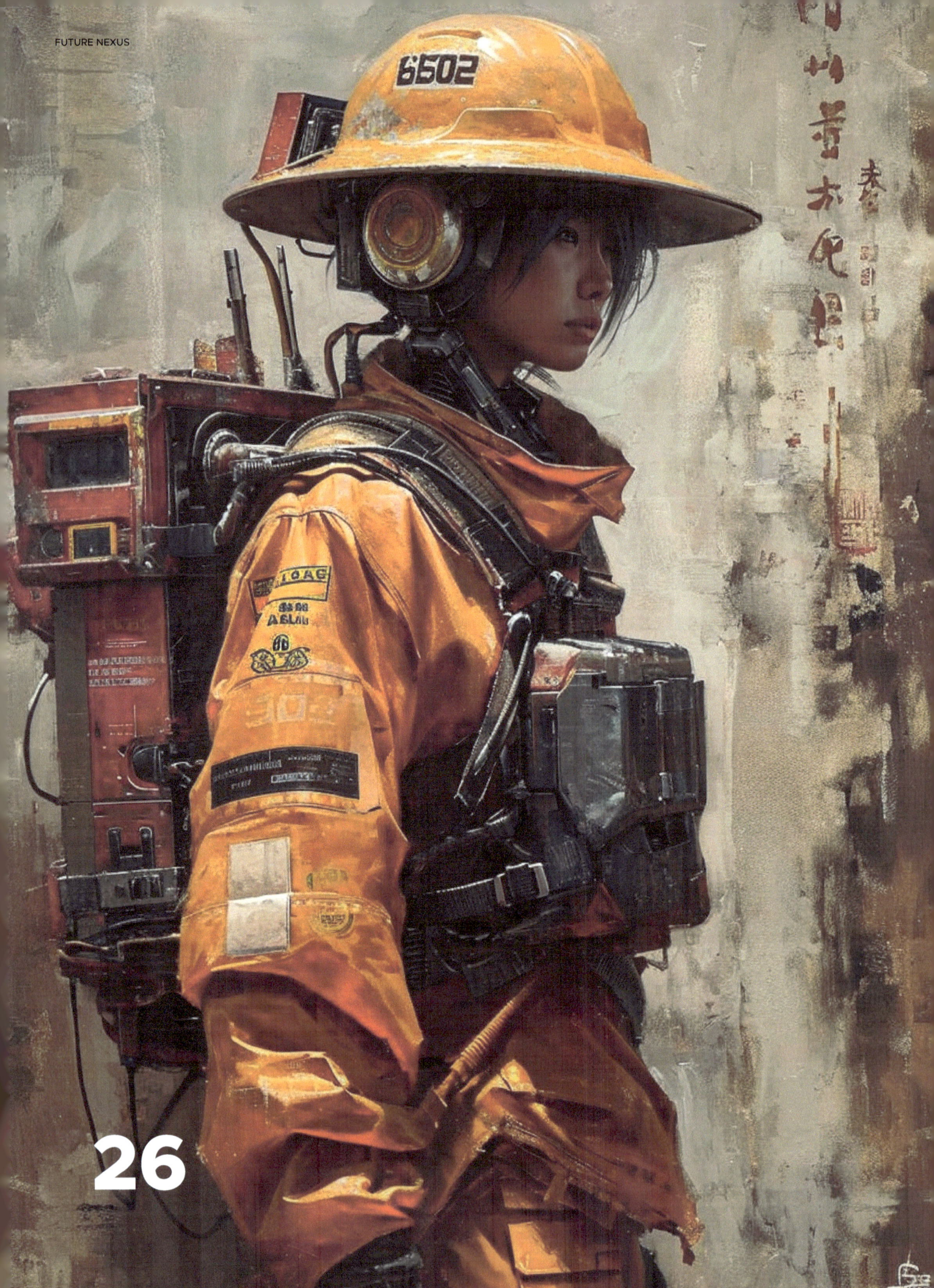

26

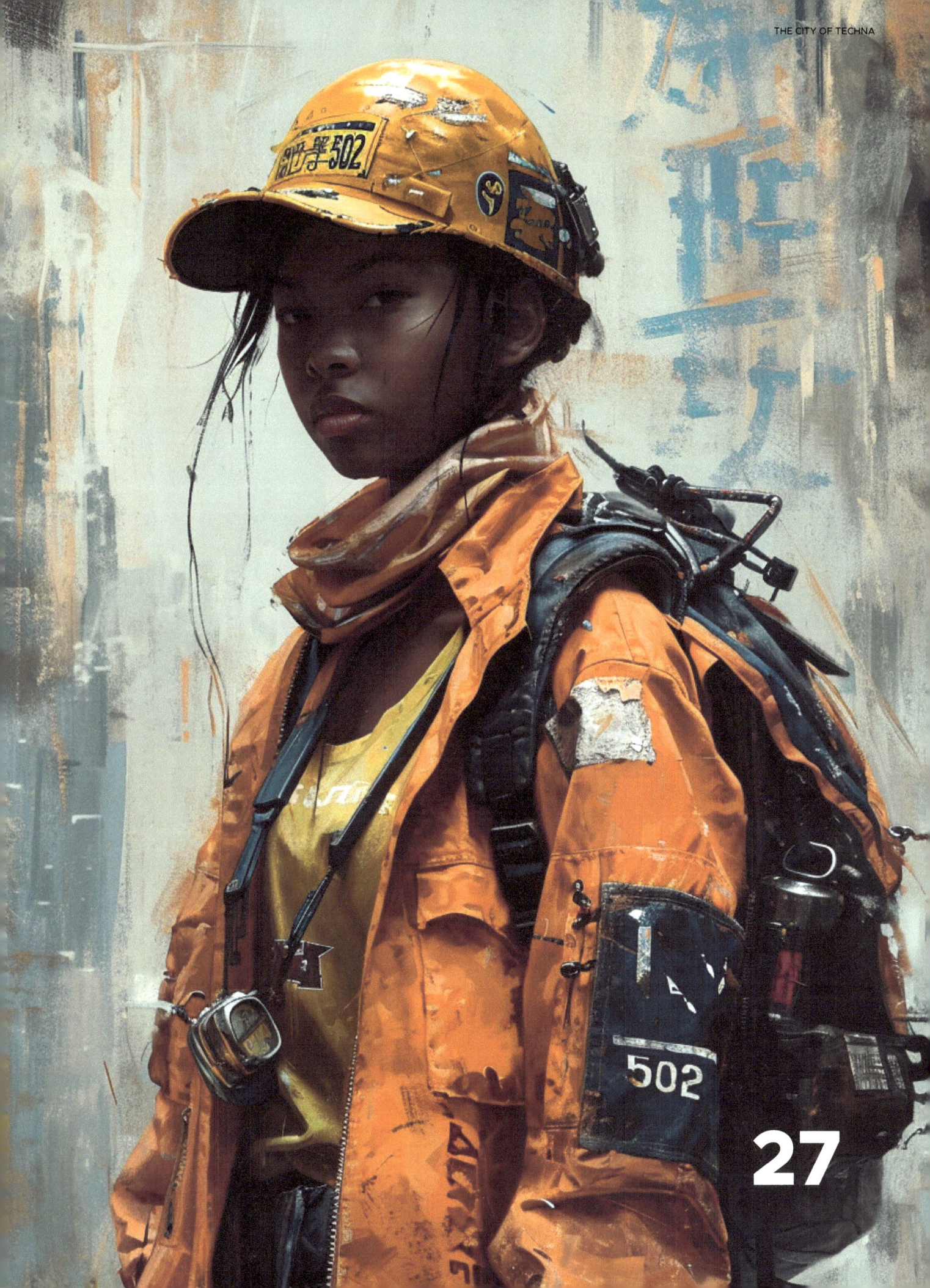

27

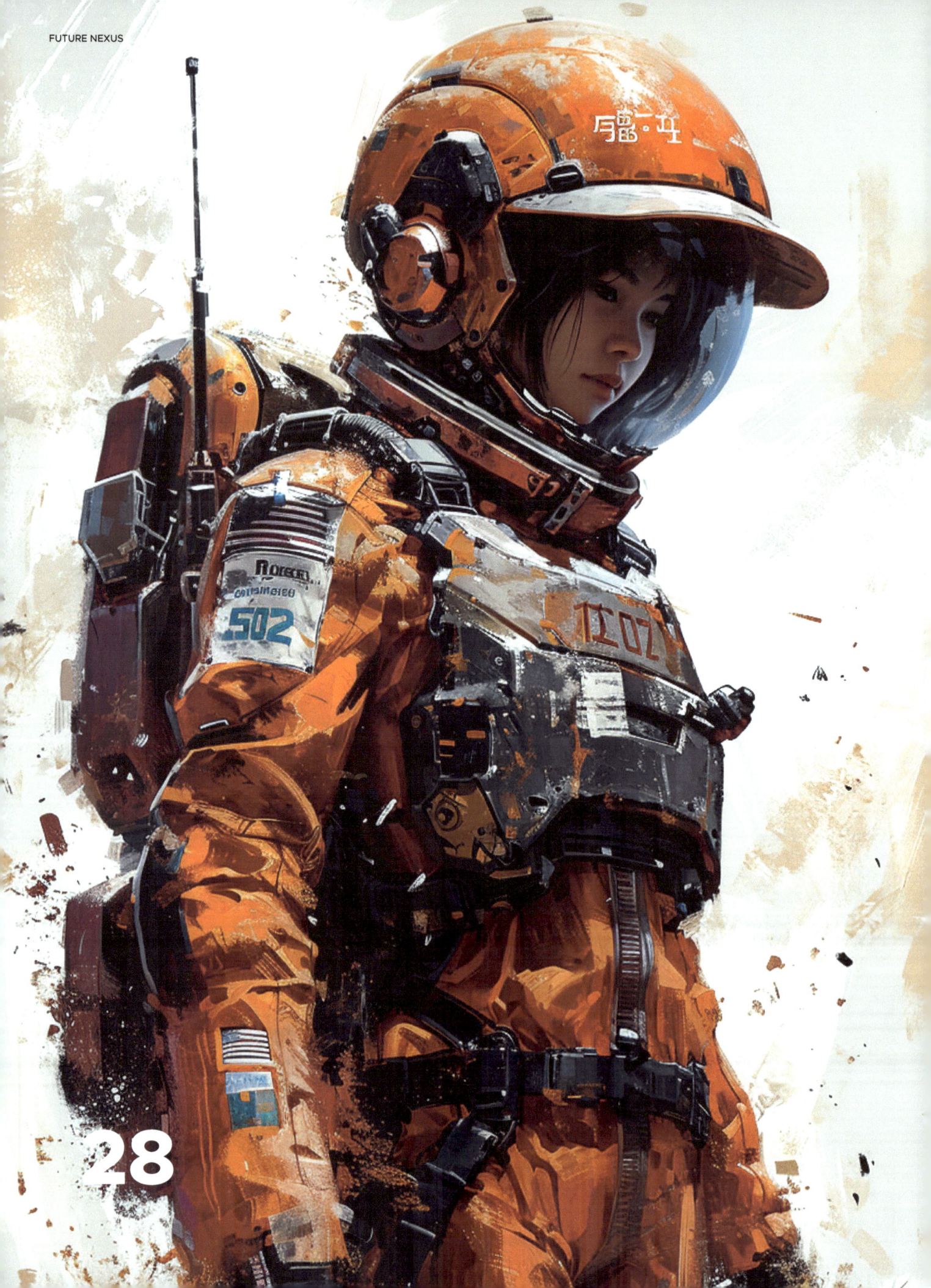

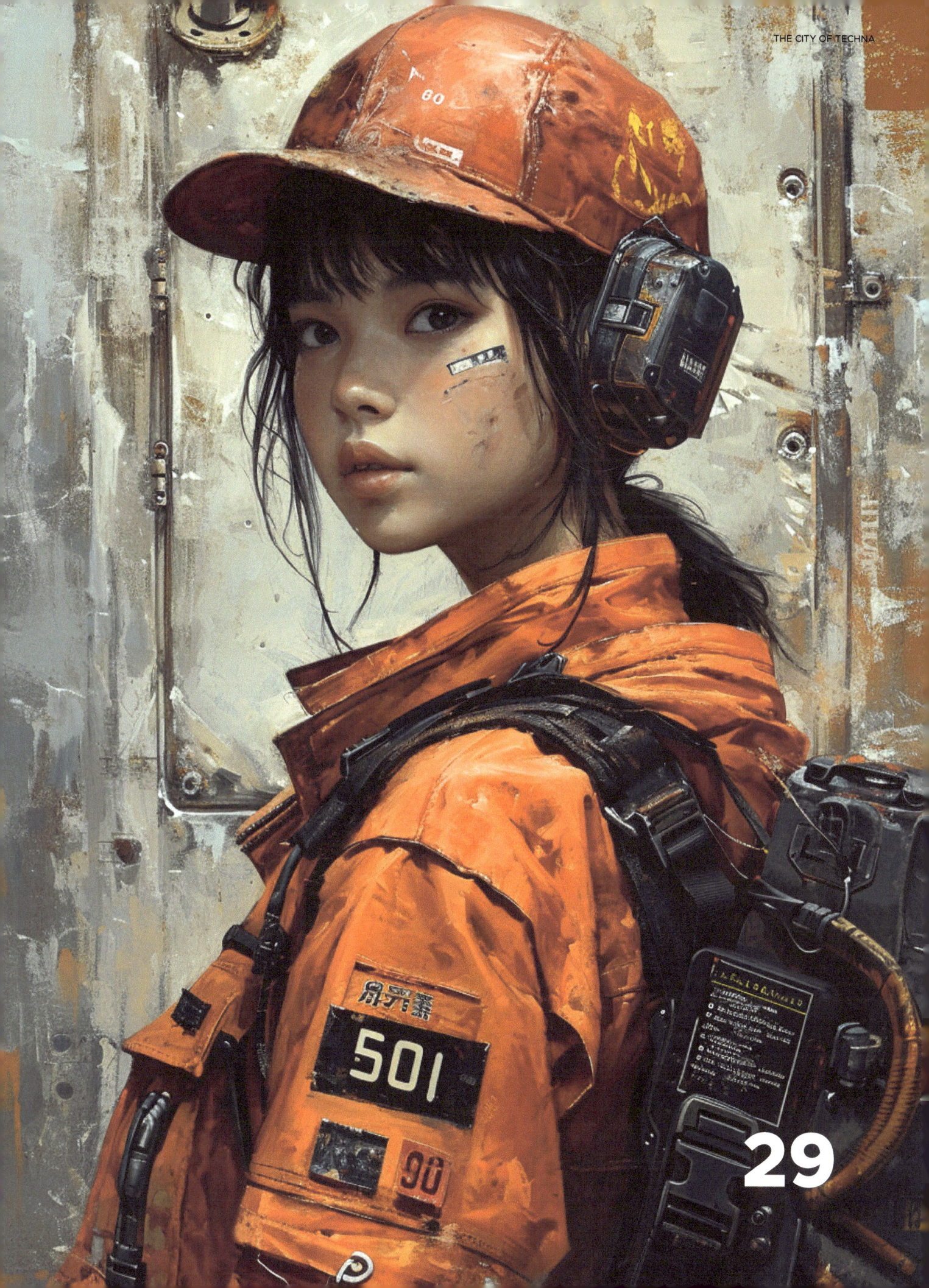

29

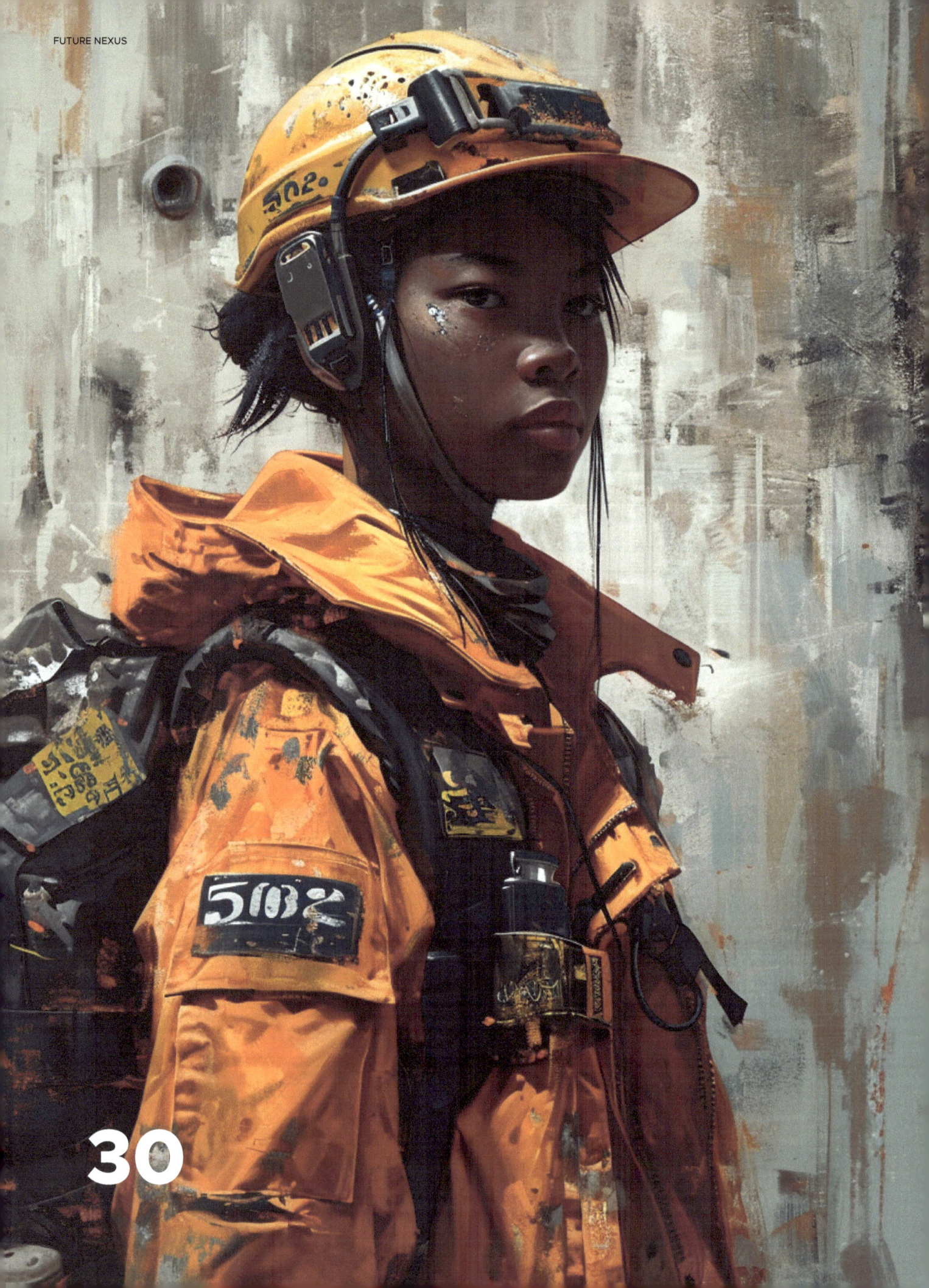

30

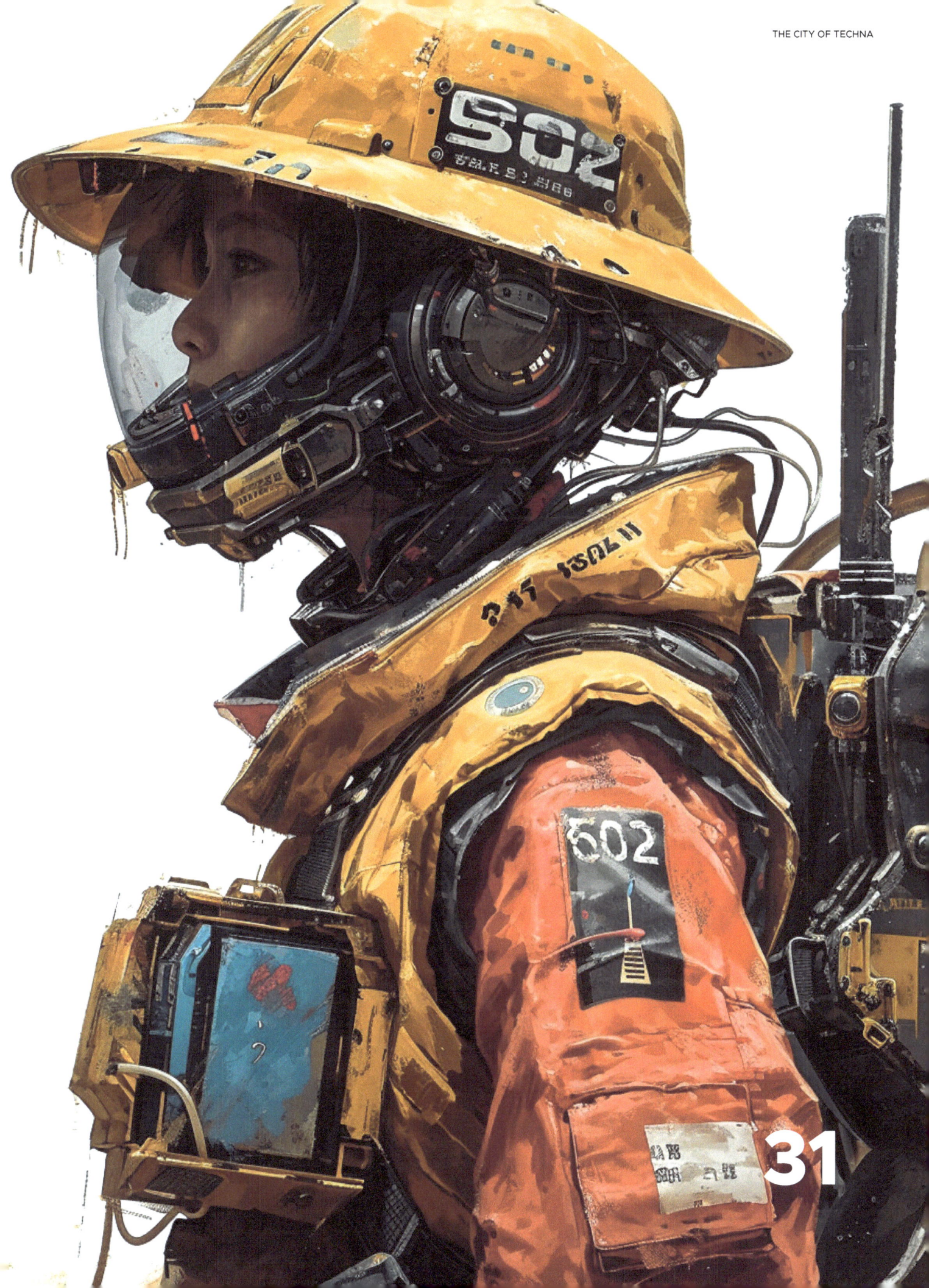

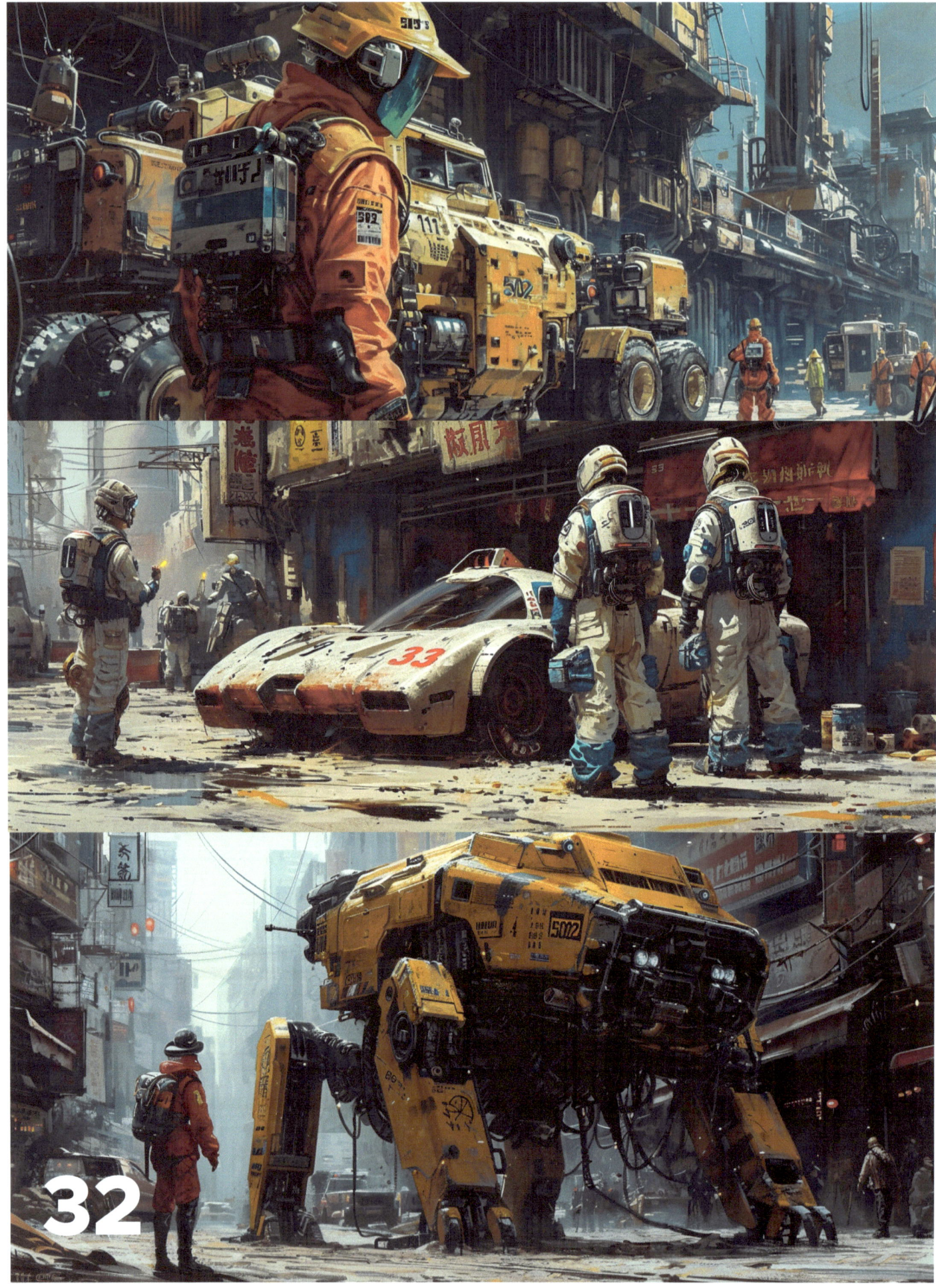

32

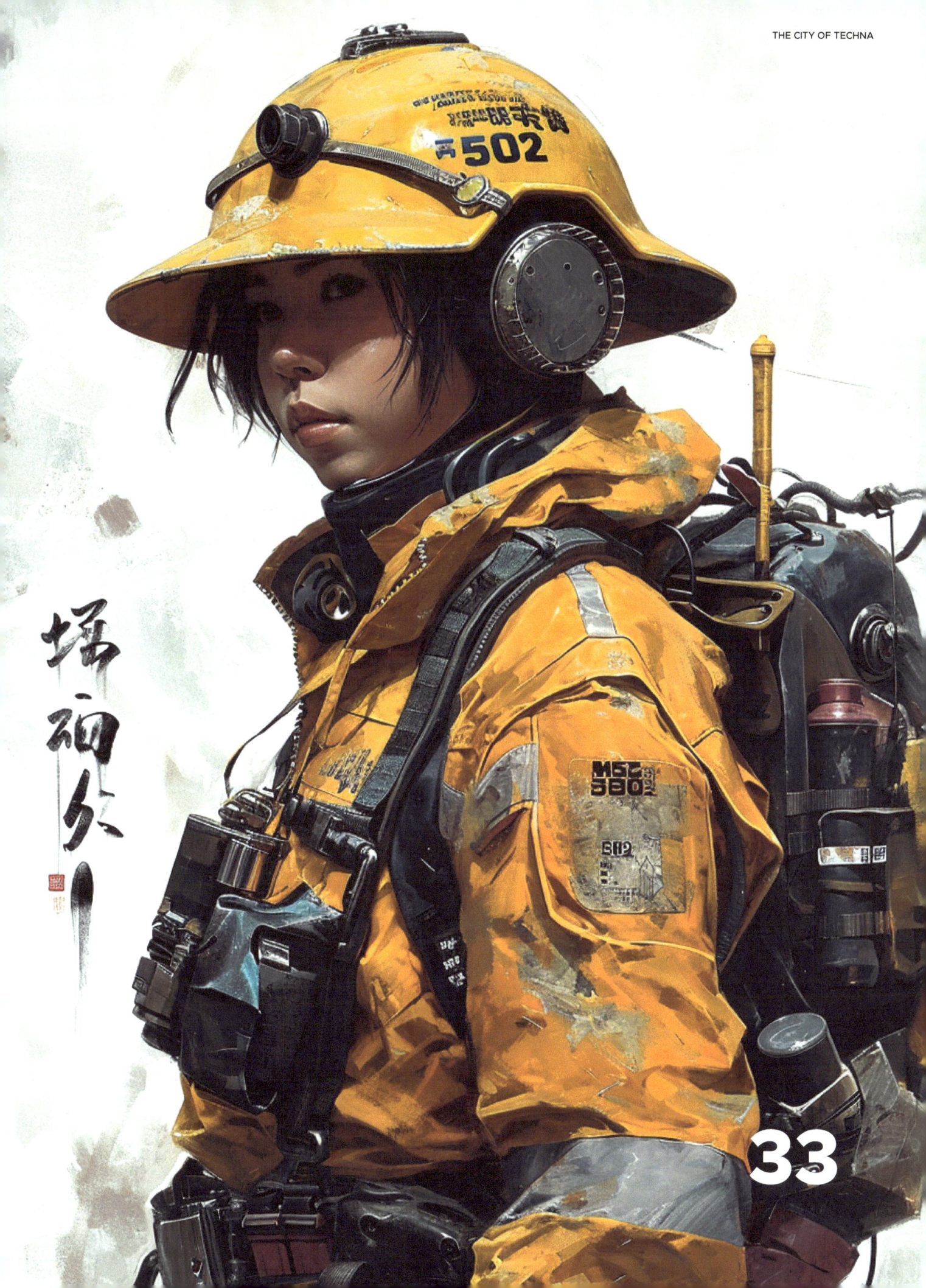

33

Dear Reader,

Thank you for embarking on this journey through the futuristic world of Techna. Your curiosity and imagination have brought life to the pages of this story, and we hope it has inspired you as much as it inspired us in its creation.

In Techna, we explore a harmonious blend of humanity and technology, showcasing the boundless possibilities of the future. Your interest and engagement are what drive these stories forward, and for that, we are deeply grateful.

We look forward to sharing more adventures with you in the future. Until then, may the spirit of innovation and progress continue to guide your path.

Warmest regards,

Emanuel Maia

www.ingramcontent.com/pod-product-compliance
Lightning Source LLC
Chambersburg PA
CBHW042029230526
45474CB00006B/53